Simon Northouse writes fiction books designed to entertain. His stories include hefty doses of self-deprecating humour, irony, farce, and droll bathos delivered in a deadpan voice. His characters leap from the page, and the plots twist and turn as he delves into the dark alcoves of modern life and the strange things we humans do. However, as many of his fans have pointed out, there is much, much more to his books than laughter and a smattering of social commentary.

He touches on issues that have plagued humans since the first man pointed at a woman on the back of a woolly mammoth and shouted, "Oi, love, come down from there. That's a man's job!" Racism, misogyny, sexism, elitism, classism, anxiety, self-doubt, hubris and entitlement are a sprinkling of topics that intersperse his works.

Keeping On Again!

Discombobulated Boxset/Omnibus Edition: Keep on Keeping On / Keep Karma and Carry On / Lockdown Diary Blues / Carry On Rewardless

Simon Northouse

FLABBERGASTED
PUBLISHING

Flabbergasted Publishing

simon@simonnorthouse.com or visit the Author's website at https://www.subscribepage.com/author_simon_northouse_home or Facebook page https://www.facebook.com/simonnorthouse

Published by Flabbergasted Publishing

First Edition

Kindle e-book ISBN-13: 978-0-6489684-7-4

Paperback ISBN-13: 978-0-6489684-8-1

Contents

Keep On Keeping On

Book 1

From the Author

Welcome to the "Discombobulated Boxset" a collection of anecdotes, reflections, true stories, and humorous musings, *(I think the reader will be the judge of that... Ed)*. By the way, the person italicised in parentheses is my editor. Well, he's not really an editor, he's a good friend of mine, (acquaintance would be a better description) who thinks he's an editor. He reads everything I write to make sure I don't go over the top and cause moral outrage to millions, *(you wish... Ed)*

Sometimes, I would like to shut him up because he can be damn annoying, but it's a cross I have to bear, *(I'm still here, you know... Ed)*

The following articles have been collated from my monthly "Discombobulated" newsletter, plus some new bonus material. This is not the sort of book you'd sit down and read in one hit. It is the type of book you would peruse while sitting on a bus, or in a waiting room or maybe even on the toilet which would make it toilet humour, *(oh, no, you've started already... Ed.)* Then again, you can read it however and wherever you like. I don't care. If you enjoy it, then why not sign-up for the "Discombobulated" newsletter and get it delivered to your inbox once a month. This link will take you to my website sign-up page.

https://www.subscribepage.com/author_simon_northouse_home

Of course, if you don't like it, there's not much I can do about it at this late stage. I'll try harder next time.

All the best and keep on keeping on!

Simon Northouse

Chapter 1

Giraffes

S ometimes, when I'm trawling the internet wasting my life, I stumble across something that makes me say, "No! That cannot be true", at which point I waste more time by doing pointless investigative research (i.e. Google it).

Just such a thing happened last week. However, before I continue—a warning. The following "mildly interesting fact" contains adult giraffe content. If you are of a delicate disposition or a giraffe, you may want to skip this section.

The headline which caught my eye was this, "The female giraffe urinates in the male giraffe's mouth as part of the mating act". Call me a traditionalist, but as courtship rituals go, it's not really my cup of tea... if you get my drift. What's wrong with wearing a figure-hugging white chiffon number, a new hairdo, and a provocative fluttering of the eyelashes to get the male libido racing? Then there's the actual act itself. How the hell does she manage it? She'd have to be a bloody good shot to hit her intended target. Does the male lay under her to make it easier? Or is he happily minding his own business under a tree, finishing the cryptic crossword when next minute he's looking up at the sky thinking,

"Hmm, they didn't forecast rain today."

All pertinent questions requiring answers. Then I had a thought. Maybe the female giraffe is kinkier than she appears to be. Although, I cannot imagine her dressed in red latex thigh boots whilst gripping a riding crop between her teeth, no matter how hard I try.

If any giraffes are reading this, please don't think I am trying to ridicule your mating habits. They may be outré but I'm a firm believer in live and let live.

After exhaustive research, I finally found the truth. Although the headline was sensationalised somewhat, it is, in fact, true. If I could write book blurbs as eye-catching as that headline, I would be an international bestseller by now. So, here are some facts.

The female Giraffe only mates when she's good and ready. She will not get it on and bang her gong with any old dropkick who happens to be passing by. She wants the most suitable male to sire her child... erm... calf. A mate with strong genes, a steady job, well-groomed and one who lowers the toilet seat when finished.

When the female giraffe goes into estrus, she releases powerful pheromones which attract males. The equivalent of a spray of Chanel Grand Extrait to the cleavage for humans. It sends Gerry Giraffe wild. The male then rubs his head against the female's bum until she urinates—don't try this at home. He then tastes the urine, rather like one would a fine wine, and if the bouquet and flavour are to his liking, he tries to mount Mrs Giraffe (or Ms Giraffe–I'm not sure where giraffes sit or stand in the emancipation stakes).

Now, she likes to play hard to get. After all, she doesn't want to appear desperate. There's nothing more off-putting than a desperate female giraffe who's in season, is there? Playing hardball may include moving forward just as the male is about to mount her, (I'd call this teasing and bloody damn annoying for the male), running away to see if he follows, ignoring his phone calls or refusing to laugh at his lame jokes. If she spots a more desirable male nearby, say, one with an extensive portfolio of blue-chip shares and a Maserati, she will rub his neck with her neck to show her preference.

Finally, when she has picked her mate, usually by asking her friends what they think of him, she is ready for the deed. She stands completely still, which is a signal to the male he may proceed. Thankfully, this signal is not replicated in the human species otherwise, there'd be many unwanted pregnancies by women standing at bus stops and riding in lifts. Once the earth has moved for him, he dismounts and buggers off despite the female Giraffe wanting to talk about what colour to paint the nursery—so there are some similarities to the human species after all.

The female is in gestation for 14 ½ months by which time she can be seen staggering across the Serengeti screaming, "get this thing out of me, I've had enough!" She gives birth to her calf standing up, which to me is more astonishing than urinating in her mate's mouth. It's a long way to fall for a newborn calf and how giraffes have survived as a species is beyond me. I'm not suggesting the giraffe should be on her back, with her legs in stirrups or floating in a birthing pool, but surely there's a better way to deliver your precious cargo than letting it drop six feet to the ground—but what do I know.

The newborn is usually up and limping around with the aid of a walking stick within an hour, wondering what in hell's name has just happened. As for the male, well, let's say he's an absentee dad, and the female rears the calf herself whilst issuing court orders to the father for calf maintenance payments and bitching about him to her pals.

Here endeth this month's "Mildly Interesting Fact". One last thing, when I started this article, I told you I was searching the internet whereupon I came across the above mind-boggling headline. I know what you are thinking, and you're wrong! I was not looking for giraffe porn! I'd actually typed into Google the phrase, "fact is stranger than fiction"... honest.

One last thing; I've just ordered a giraffe online. Not sure if it will be delivered though, I was told it's a tall order.

Chapter 2

Ants In The Pants

I've had a torrid couple of weeks. Firstly, I've been suffering from tennis elbow, and I don't even play tennis and secondly, last week I had a centipede take up residence in my underpants... while I was still in them—stop laughing—it isn't funny!

As I flopped out of bed the other morning, I felt a movement in my jocks. At first, I assumed it was the usual suspect, as I was half-asleep. However, I soon realised this was not a natural sensation; it was a wriggly, squiggly feeling. There's only one thing faster than the speed of light, and it's a man taking off his Y-fronts when he suspects a creepy-crawly is within striking distance of his family jewels. Not only that, but the malevolent little bugger had taken a couple of bites out of me. Luckily, my three sentinels in the Rapid Response Unit were unscathed, but it was a damn close call that could have resulted in serious swelling—which—could have been a blessing.

My first reaction was, "How the hell did a centipede get into my undies?" Initially, I thought it might have been a macabre practical joke played by my wife. However, a centipede is not her style—a tarantula or scorpion—yes, but not a centipede.

I'm a man with an inquisitive nature so I conducted some extensive research (Google, again) on centipedes which leads neatly on to this month's mildly interesting fact.

Despite the name, centipedes can never have exactly 100 legs. Why? Because they always have an odd number *(I'd say having that number of legs is bloody odd to start with—Ed).* They can have 99 or 101 legs but never 100, as it's an even number. Of course, they could have 100 legs if they'd lost one leg in a lawn mowing accident, I guess.

Using the internet to find out exactly how many legs a centipede possesses has proved confusing. As there are over eight thousand distinct species, this is hardly surprising. Some people say anywhere between 15 and 427, but 177 seems to crop up the most.

Centipedes are rarely seen during daylight hours as they spend most of the day in the bathroom clipping their toenails. They venture out at night looking for food and a good podiatrist. Their food of choice is meat, as I'm acutely aware, and they'll eat practically anything, including other insects, earthworms, slugs, dead rodents, and even discarded KFC... I know, it's hard to believe.

Now here's a weird thing. Reproduction for the centipede does not involve copulation, which to me is the best part of reproduction. I think someone needs to have a quiet word in the male centipede's ear and tell him he's missing a trick. I won't go into too much detail about the reproductive process as some of you may be eating, but I'll give you a quick overview.

Let's say, the male centipede takes things into his own hands or, in his case, feet, until he hits the jackpot. The more sophisticated centipede, (let's call him Raphael) will then leave his jackpot on the web of Mrs Centipede, who may or may not be amused by his offering, depending on what sort of day she's had at the office. If she's in the mood, she will embrace Raphael's deposit, and this will fertilise her egg. However, the less sophisticated male centipede, (we'll call him Dave) leaves his jackpot in any old place in the off-chance Mrs Centipede treads in it—which, with that many legs, is a distinct possibility.

So why did a centipede take up lodgings in my underpants? Apparently, they like somewhere warm and moist to curl up in to get a good day's sleep. I guess my undergarments meet those criteria. They also like to be safe and find a hidey-hole where they are unlikely to be disturbed. Once again, my undies pass that test with flying colours.

It is possible my jocks fell from the washing line and a passing centipede saw them as the arthropods equivalent of the Sky Villa at The Palms Resort. However, for that to be true, it would have meant my many-legged friend had been camping out for nearly twenty-four hours at Northouse HQ. It's conceivable but unlikely.

Excluding my wife and the camping theory, it leaves only one alternative. The little devil must have burrowed in as I slept. I only hope it was a female centipede and not a male looking for a bit of solo fun.

You may wonder what happened to the centipede *(no, not really—Ed.)* Did I kill him or her? The answer is no. Centipedes are excellent at killing other insects, such as spiders, silverfish, moths, and mosquitoes. I like to think of Mr (or hopefully Mrs) Centipede as my personal security guard, keeping me safe from a whole host of other nasties. But if the centipede goes off-piste again and crosses the border into the land of leaks and peaks, he's going to be an ex-centipede.

Lastly, here's another proven fact; did you know that if you are bitten in the groin by a centipede, you won't sing "Magic Moments" by Perry Como for over a month.

Chapter 3

The Gloat Email

I look forward to Christmas for many reasons. Eating, drinking, sleeping, arguing with the wife as we try to manoeuvre the Christmas tree into its stand, and making disparaging remarks about the Von Trapp's singing ability.

However, there is one thing I do not enjoy—the yearly Christmas "gloat" email from people I once worked with for a few weeks back in 1994. I have three people who send me these festive missives, Bob, Karen, and someone who refers to themselves simply as "Z". I cannot ever recall working or knowing anyone whose first or last name began with Z. Maybe at some point, I've exchanged email addresses with Mark Zuckerberg, Jay-Z or Zoe Ball but I don't really move in those circles—well, not anymore.

The emails give me a recap of their year, their perfect year—may I add. They gush about their gifted children, their expensive overseas trips, their work promotions. They also contain interesting nuggets of information such as, "on June 15th I had boiled eggs for breakfast with one slice of multi-grain toast." I'm not sure how I've survived this long without knowing that. In fact, now I think of it, their emails are a bit like this newsletter—WTF! *(You're not wrong there, mate—Ed.)*

I never usually reply as I don't want to encourage the buggers. However, this year, I composed my own "year of reflection" to stick it back to them, with spades. However, when my wife read my email, she said,

"Don't even think about hitting the send button—you idiot!" My reply was, "Guess what, my sweetness and light, I will let my newsletter subscribers decide, so suck on that pipe!" She responded with something like, "W**K*R!" My hearing is not the best these days, for reasons you may have already ascertained.

Here is my draft email. If I receive overwhelming support to send it, then I can enjoy a guilt free piece of schadenfreude to enjoy over Christmas.

Dear Bob, Karen, and Z,

even though you do not know each other, I am replying en masse as I can't be arsed to write to each of you individually—after all, life is short, or at least it appears that way after reading your emails.

It's amazing to think three such disparate people have so much in common. You are all super successful, (which really is astonishing as, Bob and Karen, when I knew you, you were bottom of the food chain and sinking fast—and Z—I don't even know who the hell you are). Apparently, you all have children who are "gifted" and "beautiful". I'm sorry, Bob, but I think you may be gilding the Lilly slightly there. As I recall, if it's the correct Bob, you looked like the half-cousin of Quasimodo after a hard night on the bells. I cannot imagine your daughter is a younger version of Nicole Kidman, as you claim if she was sired from your spawn.

Anyway, I'd love to shake each one of you warmly by the throat and here is my email reflecting on my year—for a change.

WOW! What a year!!!!! My, how time flies. It seems like only twelve months ago since I was sitting here reading your self-obsessed, vainglorious twaddle. Now it's time for my egotistical ramblings.

On 30th December 2017, I married my long-suffering life partner, Mavis. It was a very special day as not only did we tie the knot, but I also found my precious Swiss Army Penknife stuck behind the bar fridge in the shed! Imagine my surprise. It was the highlight of the day. Everyone laughed and laughed, well, almost everyone.

We had so many guests I lost count after five. My, how they ate and drank, and ate and drank, and ate and drank. Of course, it is a once in a lifetime occasion, (fingers crossed ha, ha,) so I wasn't counting the cost (£154.89 - excluding the ice). However, I must admit it slightly miffed me when I found out some rotter helped themself to a few bottles from my vintage wine collection of Merda Vino 2018. At £0.49 per bottle, it's not something to be swilled like beer! I never caught the culprit, (good job I didn't! I was bloody ropeable on the day). However, Mavis's mother was particularly happy and boisterous on the night, which was somewhat out of character for her—not that I'm pointing an accusatory finger (I still have the scars from the last time I made that mistake).

We received many lovely gifts we will treasure for a while. I didn't know you could get such quality at the £1 Shop.

Not long after the wedding, I had a terrible accident when I snicked my cuticle while clipping my big toenail. Unless you have experienced this traumatic and life-changing event, you have absolutely no idea what pain is. Give me childbirth any day of the week! However, I was rather puzzled by the paramedic's less than sympathetic attitude. I immediately lodged a formal complaint with the hospital and justice was swiftly administered. They were stood down for two weeks without pay.

Yes, I know you all want to hear about my work life. Well, nothing much has changed there. I'm steering the ship, managing my workload and everyone else's, cutting costs, raising profits, and smashing all the benchmarks I set last year. I'm still the Senior Manager, although my title of "Office Clerk" doesn't truly reflect the enormity of my responsibilities or my natural genius for the role. However, I'm not one to quibble over titles, although I would prefer it if people referred to me as "Sir" rather than the more informal, noggin. (I must Google the word noggin and find out its meaning. I'm sure it must be Nordic for king or warrior leader or such like).

My eldest daughter, Cleetoris, will start at the (exclusive) Grammar School this year (we had to decline the Scholarship to King's College, as she didn't like the colour of the school uniform). As you will be aware, scholarships are awarded only to the most gifted and intelligent children. My, oh my, it was a tough test. Over seven hundred applicants from all over the country turned up for it. I really didn't think Cleetoris had a chance, but as usual, she astounded me by getting 99.9% in the test and came top. I told her not to get complacent; 99.9% is good, but there's still plenty of scope for improvement. She is looking forward to it with great excitement and anticipation. Every night when I pass her room, I hear her sobs of joy and the words "Oh, the Grammar, the Grammar, why me?"

On a rather sad note... Cleetoris has given up the piano!!!! I can hear your collective gasps and groans. I know, I know, it is a tragedy! It truly is a significant loss to the music world, and I think we should stop for a minute's silence:

Where did it all go wrong? To be fair to Cleetoris, I had some sympathy for her. Once she had mastered the complete works of Mozart, Beethoven, Chopin, Schubert, and Barry Manilow, she asked herself the question Alexander the Great asked himself after he'd conquered the known world, "Where to now? There's nothing left". I endured a similar experience as a boy of 28 when I finally mastered the Rubik's Cube after fifteen years of trying.

Her music teacher (ha, that's a contradiction in terms) had to be sedated for two days on hearing the news. I told Cleetoris she should start composing her own works, something with a bit more depth than the classics (I always found Mozart a little twee for my tastes). Alas, you can lead a horse to water, but you can't pass an eye through a camel's needle. Anyway, she's taken up the harp and viola and is already better than her tutor (who is ex-Philharmonic Symphony).

My Great Uncle Charlie, (whom none of you know) had a bunion operated on last week. I'm sure you'll all join me in wishing him the best.

The morning of May 12th was not a good one. As I got out of bed, I stubbed my big toe. I immediately had a giddy turn and had to lie down in a darkened room with a wet flannel over my forehead for three hours. I received scant sympathy from my wife, Mavis.

Unfortunately, during the year I had an argument with my local butcher when I questioned the girth of his sausage. Things became heated rather quickly. I would rather not talk about it, as I still carry the mental scars to this day. Mavis had a devil of a job removing the sausage stains from my underwear.

On June 16th, I changed the fan belt on the Toyota Hilux. Modern engines are now all computerised and extraordinarily complex. They are only supposed to be worked on by the most experienced of mechanics. However, being a bit of a handyman, I tackled the job myself. I quickly speed-read the 800-page manual and thirty minutes later, Bob's your uncle, Aunts your fanny—fanbelt fitted. I also tweaked the turbo-injectors while I was at it and replaced the big end.

We holidayed at Grimesore Bottom this year, which for those of you who haven't visited, is rather like Tuscany but with drive-through off-licences and heroin injecting rooms. We had a wonderful time making fun of the locals. Unfortunately, it was marred by the engine blowing up on the Toyota Hilux. Let me tell you, Toyota HQ would have been quaking in their boots the day they opened my letter! We settled out of court (I'm not a litigious person) and I'm now the proud owner of a Toyota drinks bottle and keyring. (I've actually attached the keyring to my Swiss Army Knife, as I'm a bit of a joker—ha, ha!)

Daughter number 2, Vaginna, was made Student of the Year at kindergarten. I've told her she needs to hide her talents under a bushel a little more as she's making all the other kids look like real thickos. She asked me what a bushel was—she's such a prankster.

I think some of the other parents have developed a touch of the green-eyed monster, as they seem to avoid me when I go to collect her. It can't be easy spawning extremely average children, but let me tell you, it's no walk in the park trying to keep up with two outrageously gifted daughters either.

I had some bad news from overseas during the year. My best mate from primary school, "Sludgebucket" was killed in a combine-harvester accident. I haven't actually spoken or written to him for over 35 years, but he will always be with me. I intended to send a wreath to his family but couldn't for the life of me remember his real name (what a klutz, ha, ha!) Mavis didn't think it appropriate to deliver a wreath to grieving parents that read, "Sludgebucket RIP". I couldn't see a problem with it, but Mavis is a little more tactful than I on these matters.

In June, Mavis spent three days in the gynaecological unit of the local hospital. Luckily, it was not contagious, and I escaped unscathed (phew!!!!)

On September 6th, we had a family outing to Kmart. The weather was fantastic, and I bought myself a new state-of-the-art plasma TV, a new iBook, and a new set of golf clubs. Mavis got herself a heavy-duty treadmill and a new girdle. However, the trip was marred by unacceptable behaviour from the girls. They asked if they could have something as well. You know me and there's no way I'll stand for that self-obsessed, materialistic, me-me-me attitude. After screaming at them for ten minutes and publicly humiliating them, I think they saw the error of their ways. I told them there would be no more family excursions for the foreseeable future if this is the thanks I get.

On the sporting front, we've tried to curtail some of the children's activities. The head scout for the British Olympic Committee put pressure on us to send Cleetoris to the Olympic Summer School during the holidays, but we stood our ground. We felt training for the 100m, 200m,

400m, 800m and 1500m in both swimming and running and the javelin, long jump, triathlon, archery, equestrian, not to mention the Marathon, was a tad too much.

As for Vaginna, she was invited to train with the English Women's Cricket Team to prepare for the next world cup. I can't help feeling that at six years old, she is a little young to be competing competitively. They'll just have to do without her batting average of 199.7.

On October 24th, I cleaned out my shed and went to the tip. Mavis slept late until 11 am and we rounded the day off nicely with a bowl of my handmade pasta and my homemade rabbit cheese (it's not easy milking rabbits, I can tell you).

Mavis has gone from strength to strength in her job and I can see the day very shortly when she'll be Head Principal. She can then start implementing her lifelong plan to revolutionise the entire education system (which is long overdue, may I add!) Her relentless discourse to the Minister for Education seems to have fallen on deaf eyes. There's none as blind as those who can't hear. However, until then she'll struggle valiantly on as assistant cleaner at Crudthorpe College.

She's now Team Leader at weight watchers and practically runs the meetings. She has lost an incredible 22 kg during the year and only gained 24 kg in return. I think it's a sterling effort and it won't be long before she'll be able to walk without serious chaffing to her inner thighs and buttocks.

Did I mention Cleetoris has taken up sculpture? Well, she has. I wasn't impressed with her first attempt, as it was a replica of Michelangelo's "David". To be honest, it was far superior to the original, but that's not the point I'm trying to make. I told her, "There's no room for plagiarism in this house". Thankfully, she heeded the message and is now working on a giant slab of marble, chiselling out the complete DNA helix of the Patagonian Dragonfly. A little obvious, I know, but at least it's her own work.

On November 30th I paid a visit to the local pharmacy to buy some Anusol as my piles have returned with a raging vengeance. I also picked up an extra-large box of panty pads for Mavis.

Well, that's all I have time for at the moment. I must dash as I am giving a headline speech at the Royal Society of Shovel Admirers this evening. It should prove to be a fascinating night as my soliloquy examines the evolution of the shovel, followed by a health and safety talk on how to turn sods correctly and lastly, the importance of having a well-oiled shaft.

We really must stay connected more often and anytime you're passing, please call in as we love visitors dropping in unannounced.

All the best from Northouse Mansions and my sincerest sympathy to you all. Go in peace.

Chapter 4

English Versus American

I t's been a hectic month with the release of a new book, working on the next one, marketing the damned things and trying to find out what was causing a revolting smell in my fridge.

Let's start with the important matters first. You'll be pleased to know I found out what was causing the eye-watering, gut-churning smell or maybe you don't really give a toss. Anyway, after forensic analysis, I eventually found the culprit—cauliflower rice. For reasons best known to herself, my wife has become obsessed with cauliflower rice. What is wrong with "rice" rice? Two packets in the crisper were only a month past their sell-by date, which in our house usually means, "Ah, it'll be all right." Not on this occasion! After I had donned radioactive personal protection, gas mask, Geiger counter and extinguished all naked flames, I removed the life-threatening culprits from the fridge and deposited them in the outside bin.

However, as I write this, bin collection is still two days away, and it is damned hot outside. My nearest neighbour lives about two miles away and he called around this morning to ask if I had noticed a "violent miasma in the air." I feigned ignorance and declared I had noticed nothing untoward —which is hard to do while holding your breath. The only positive to take from this is the bin will walk itself down the driveway in a couple of days, so saving me the trouble.

Okay, so let's quickly move on to this month's "Mildly Interesting Fact".

I occasionally receive emails from kind people who tell me there is a spelling error in one of my books. I appreciate this as I'm always looking for perfection, *(but surprisingly, never finding it—Ed)*. However, on most occasions, it is not a spelling error but the difference between "British" English and "American" English.

Being a native-born Yorkshire man and therefore English and also British and a citizen of the United Kingdom and the British Isles and a member of the Commonwealth (it's complicated), I speak and write in British English. In fact, it was only with the advent of Microsoft Windows in the early nineties I became aware there was such a thing as American English. Until that time, I assumed there was only English English.

Microsoft Word would always let me know when I had misspelt (or misspelled) "colour", indicating it is spelt (or spelled) "color". It would also get annoyed with me for "specialising" instead of "specializing", or for using the unit of measurement known around the world as "metre" instead of meter. It once even picked me up for spelling "socks" incorrectly, insisting the correct spelling was indeed, "sox"—proving Microsoft and computers have a sense of humour or humor, as obviously, no one would ever spell socks as sox.

This got me thinking, *(always a bad sign—Ed)*, about the British and Americans. We have much in common and yet—we are very different.

One of the biggest differences is our units of measurement. Britain used the imperial system until the early seventies. When we joined the Common Market (think European Union), we converted to metric (reluctantly). Gone were pounds and ounces, miles, and feet, square yards, shillings, groats, fathoms, and tons. These were replaced with grams, kilograms, metres, and centimetres. In addition, we had a new decimal currency, which has 100 pence (pennies) in a pound (instead of the more logical 240?). However, it has never sat comfortably with the nation. We still serve beer in pints, not litres. We fill our cars up in gallons and we still curse in imperial.

"He's a six-foot waste of space."

"I'll bet you a pound to a penny of shit he's wrong!" and

"He's a few bob short of a shilling."

The USA employs the imperial system of measurement, but here is a "mildly interesting fact". In the US (and I think Canada) a ton is equal to 2000 pounds, whereas, in Britain, a ton is equal to 2240 pounds. These differences in units of measurement are easy to sort out by using an online converter.

Where the real confusion lies is in our use of language—which, if you haven't fallen asleep by now—is where I started.

Talking of Canadians, I once had an American tell me a Canadian was simply an American without a sense of humour—a bit harsh, I thought. That was until I spent two weeks on a coaching—camping holiday around the outback of Australia (not Austria) in the company of two Canadians. They weren't miserable by any means, but I did not see them laugh once during the fortnight! I found this most peculiar as there's a lot to laugh at whilst on a coaching holiday in Australia—the Australians for starters *(oops, there go all your Australian and Canadian subscribers—Ed).* No, really, I love the Australians. They have a great sense of humour and can laugh at themselves and the British, well, mainly the British. They also change their Prime Minister more often than I change my underwear, which probably says more about me than it does about them.

Okay, so where was I? Ah yes, that's right, I've just lost all my Canadian and Australian subscribers and now I'll probably lose all my American ones.

Let me start at the top by beginning at the bottom. In the States, a "fanny" is a colloquial term for a bottom, behind, buttocks. However, in Britain, a fanny is not a bottom. It's pretty damn close to a bottom, and I must confess it is a very pleasant place to visit, although I don't get there as often as I'd like. So, if you're an American visiting Britain, I would advise against using the following statements in public places in case you are arrested.

"Here, hand me the cucumber, I'll stick it in my fanny pack."

"If you don't stop messing around young lady, you'll get a smacked fanny!"

"I'm sorry officer, but all I did was slap my wife on the fanny..." at which point you'll be handcuffed and thrown into the back of a divvy wagon (police van) and whisked away. I think by now you may understand what a fanny is in the UK.

Here's a statement for you, "I'm pissed!" Americans reading this will assume I am extremely annoyed, maybe even angry. The British will look at their watches, and think,

"Bloody hell, he's started a bit early, hasn't he? I think he has a drinking problem." Brits, when pissed, are usually found staggering down the high street at 2 am singing "Oh what a lovely bunch of coconuts", whilst eating a kebab and looking for someone to fight.

In Britain, we wee. In the States, they pee. We wee in a toilet unless we're pissed, then we wee in a shop doorway. Americans do their peeing in a bathroom or "John". I'm not entirely sure how John reacts to this, but I assume he's used to it by now.

In Britain, our normal greeting is "all right" usually said as "arite". Although, in Yorkshire, we use a mixture of "arite" and "eh up", as we are slightly more sophisticated than the rest of the country. The Americans seem to use, "Hi, how are you doing?" as their preferred greeting. I would advise against using this term in the UK as you may get a, "What the bloody hell has it got to do with you?" thrown back in your face. I would also stay away from the greeting, "Howdy" as you will either be laughed at or the person you said it to will begin a bad impersonation of John Wayne.

Unlike Americans, the Brits rarely complain, even when the service or food is appallingly bad, which is most of the time. We vent our spleen by whispering to our partner in the restaurant,

"Well, we won't be coming here again, thank you very much!" When asked by the waiter if everything is "arite," we reply,

"Yes, yes, it's all fine, wonderful, thanks". The Brits also talk quietly in public places unless we are pissed, then we get an overwhelming desire to speak at American volume, i.e. deafening. Although to be fair, most Americans I have met have been from Texas or New York—if I spoke to someone, from say, Wisconsin or Idaho, would I still need to wear double hearing protection?

America's head of state (The President) is democratically elected by the people every four years and can only serve a maximum of two terms, presumably to stop the abuse of power—a wise move. However, the British head of state is based on genealogy and gender and inherits the position from their parents (i.e. the King or Queen). There is no election process, no democratic voting, and they hold the position for life, unless they do something foolish, like marrying an American divorcee, at which point they will be forced to abdicate and the next in "line" will take up the mantle.

Of course, the US President is not only the head of state but also the head of government and wields enormous power. In fact, it is probably the most powerful position in the world. The Queen of England, Britain, and the Commonwealth does not really have any power. She is part of what is called a constitutional monarchy.

The British have a peculiar tendency to insist on using utensils to eat their food. For our American cousins, let me explain. These utensils replace the fingers and are called, "knife, fork, and spoon". Each one has a different use and I'm sure if you've ever visited Britain then you may have spotted these strange looking objects in restaurants, sorry, diners.

In Britain, we have servings of small, medium, and large. In America, there is no direct equivalent to the British small—it does not exist. They have regular (i.e. British large), large and extra-large. In fact, I figure (or reckon) that in the next twenty years, the word "small" will have disappeared from the American language—and British English will be called American American.

Let's talk about herbs. The British pronounce the "H" in herbs. As in "Herbie Goes To Monte Carlo". If it were meant to be pronounced "erbs" it would be spelt "erbs". The same assessment goes for "oregano" (or-eee-gar-no) and "basil" (baaz-ill)—not"o-regin-no" or "bay-zil".

When it comes to cars (or automobiles), things get really confusing. Brits call it a gear stick, not a shift stick. A bonnet is a hood, a boot is a trunk, and a bumper is a fender. However, a bonnet is also knitted headwear, and a trunk can be a valise, or suitcase, or part of a tree or an elephant's nose, or a euphemism for a penis. If someone asks you,

"Would you like to see my elephant impression?" Politely decline and walk away.

A boot is also a type of footwear, and we also boot a footy ball and we can also get a boot to the balls, usually when we are pissed, at 2 am, looking for a fight, eating a kebab and singing—"Oh what a lovely bunch..." well, you get the picture.

The Americans "hood" could also refer to a gangster or your neighbourhood or neighborhood. Our gangster is also a gangster, but we call him the taxman.

I'm not sure if Americans have an unhealthy preoccupation with the weather, but in Britain, we do. We talk about the weather constantly, which is surprising really, as for 363 days of the year it is grey (gray) skies with a touch of drizzle and a bit on the "chilly side". When Britain has a scorching summer, (e.g. 3 continuous days of 27°C / 81°F) the entire country goes into party mode. We use it as another excuse to get pissed.

The British have a good understanding of geography. We know the difference between Austria and Australia, Japan and China, Myanmar and

Burma. I think this innate knowledge of the countries of the world stems from the fact that at some point in our history we invaded at least one-third of them. Of course, in those days, it wasn't called invasion. It was rather quaintly known as colonisation—although I'm not sure the locals saw it that way.

The Americans don't do invasion, they do liberation, but not as well as the Brits used to do colonisation. However, Americans are smart! They realised a long time ago there's no point taking over a country unless you are going to make a dollar out of it—so they did it with their business acumen. What country in the world does not have an Apple Mac, an MS Office program, an iPad, an Intel processor? I would bet every nation on the planet has a Harley Davidson, a Jeep, a Ford, or a GM car powering down their roads right now. Which country in the world does not use Google, Amazon, and Facebook, eat from a MacDonald's, KFC, Dunkin' Donuts, or get a coffee from a Starbucks. I won't even touch on Hollywood, Netflix, Fox, or M.A.S.H.

The Americans conquered the world via the backdoor and made a very healthy profit doing so. How do the British compare? Well, over the last fifty years we have given the world—erm, erm, ah yes! We have given the world Dyson vacuum cleaners and Gordon Ramsay, so we are nearly on par.

Enough of the differences, let's look at the similarities between the two nations.

The Brits gave you, The Beatles, The Stones, The Who, The Kinks, Oasis, Rod Stewart, and Elton John. In return, the Americans gave us Chuck Berry, Elvis, Bob Dylan, Otis Redding, Sam Cook, The Doors, Motown, Eminem, The Byrds, and Mariah Carey (thanks for that).

The differences are many—but the similarities are greater still. I hope you have taken this as it was intended—a bit of tongue-in-cheek banter—

and if not, tough titty, and I think that particular phrase is common to both British and American English.

Thought to self: *Okay, let me count up. I'll lose all Canadian subscribers because they don't have a sense of humour. I'll lose both Australians because they hate the Poms (British) anyway, and I'll lose at least 600 Americans because they just love subscribing and unsubscribing. I'll also lose 3 British subs because they came home pissed and didn't know what they were doing. That leaves the guy from South Africa, the Lady-boy from Indonesia (I'll PM you soon—promise) and Snorg from Norway—so all good, onwards and upwards.*

Chapter 5

Remember the Days of the Old School Yard

Welcome to the Marbruary edition of the Discombobulated Newsletter.

"What medication is this guy on?" I hear you exclaim. What the hell is Marbruary? Well, it's a mash-up of March and February. It's a new month I've invented so I can meet my deadlines without feeling defeated. Aw, come on, cut me some slack here. Anyway, count your blessings. I was considering calling it "Farch" which sounds like a disgusting sexual practice *(and if it isn't, then it should be—Ed)*.

Note to self: *Google the word "farch" before hitting the send button otherwise, I could have 600 morally outraged readers hitting unsubscribe. For crying out loud! What is wrong with the world? Okay, forget I ever mentioned Farch.*

Time seems to be passing at an exponential rate. Do you realise it's only 10 months until Xmas? Thought that would cheer you up. So, what have I been up to since we last spoke? Well, I published the second instalment of The School Reports in early Feb. This is a humorous peek back to yesteryear when teachers were... how can I put this nicely... when they were more "robust" in their report writing. In fact, they were more robust at everything.

These were the days when schools were run like schools, i.e. prison camps, unlike today where they are more like multinational corporations. Reading my own children's reports these days means having on hand a copy of the "Dictionary Of Wank Words" to help me decipher exactly what the teacher is trying to say. Does anyone know what "horizontal integration" means? I assumed it meant lying down on the floor during a school assembly—but apparently not.

I'm certainly not having a dig at teachers. They must have one of the hardest jobs on the planet dealing with tantrums, subterfuge, aggression, and truculence—and that's just from the parents and other teachers.

As I wrote "The School Reports" it brought back a lot of memories from my school days which got me thinking about how much things have changed. This led me to do a bit of research via the big "G" in the sky (I mean Google, not God. Although, some people would say they are the same thing; omnipotent, omnipresent, omniscient, and omnidirectional— that's a lot of omnis for one newsletter, which is ominous). Anyway, I digress. This month's "Mildly Interesting Fact" is all about the old school days. So, let us take a trip back in time and revisit what it was actually like in the 50s, 60s, 70s, and 80s.

Here's a mildly interesting fact: "Margaret Thatcher" was a woman. Now, as facts go, that one is pretty lame. It's like saying water is wet. For those who have never heard of Mrs T, she was the first British female prime minister, coming to power in 1979 until her own party deposed her in 1990. However, well before then, she came to prominence in 1970 as Secretary of State for Education and Science. She became rather unpopular, as one of her first acts was to abolish the "free" milk program for 7 to 11 year olds. This got her the nickname Thatcher the Milk Snatcher.

When I started school, they gave us a small bottle of milk at morning playtime (recess), about a third of a pint. My greatest ambition was to become a milk monitor, an ambition never fulfilled and still rankles with me to this day. The milk monitor would depart about twenty minutes before playtime and would collect the empty bottles afterwards, meaning he would miss a good hour of the school day. I say "he", as yes, in those days there was a clear demarcation about what was appropriate for each gender.

These were also the days of corporal punishment. I'm sure many of you will remember this, but for those who are a lot younger and don't fully understand the concept—let me explain. Corporal punishment involved a fully grown man or woman beating the shit out of a defenceless small child with impunity.

I well remember the day I was caught fighting with another boy in the school playground. Unfortunately, Mr Crowbottom (I kid you not) was on yard duty. Old Birdbum (as he was known to the kids) was the fearsome headmaster who ruled with an iron rod. He marched us to his office by twisting and dragging us by the ears. If you've never had your ear twisted sharply, try it one day, it's great fun.

I knew we would both be getting the cane or the slipper. However, old Birdbum was a master of psychological warfare. He wouldn't take us into his office and quickly lecture us, then dole out the punishment—oh no! That would be too quick. He made us wait in his reception room until playtime was over, by which time he would have rounded up at least another ten boys for some petty misdemeanours. These could range from swearing, fighting, accidental damage to school property, chewing gum, or even picking your nose in public.

The waiting was the worst. For some boys, it was their first time, and they would sit, sweating, with tears rolling down their cheeks, asking if it was going to hurt. There was one lad called Jimmy Broadbent who was older than me, and I reckon he spent more time in the reception room than he did studying in class. He was an old hand, and it was always heartening to see his happy, smiling face. He would laugh, joke around, and do Birdbum impressions to get everyone laughing as we awaited the inevitable.

When we were finally summoned into his office, he would make us stand rigidly with our hands by our sides, as if we were in the army. He would light a cigarette (yes, I know, hard to believe now), sit in his chair and eye us both silently for a few seconds. Birdbum never wanted to know the whys and wherefores of a situation. No, he would jump straight to his summation and sentencing. I remember the exact words he said that day, the irony of which did not pass me by even though I was only nine years old. He said, "This school and society will not tolerate violent and aggressive behaviour." He stood, grabbed his slipper from a draw, bent us over and gave us six of the best on the backside. As I walked from the room, smarting, I remember thinking, "And who's going to give that bastard the slipper for his violent and aggressive behaviour".

If you have never been whacked on the arris by an old slipper, why not try it. Just ask your local neighbourhood sadist to administer the punishment and I can guarantee that you will not use the phrase, "Hmm, I fancy a pickled onion with that", for over a week.

We were lucky it was the slipper. It could have been the cane. The pain from a slipper thrashing dissipates in a few minutes, whereas the pain of the cane would last hours. That was a formally organised punishment administered by a kangaroo court. However, my class teachers delivered less formal punishment swiftly. This could include a slap to the head, the dreaded ear twist, the ruler to an outstretched palm or worse to the back of the knuckles; the blackboard ruler to the back of the thighs, the blackboard rubber thrown at the head, and almost every teacher had a slipper in their desk drawer.

I cannot recall a female teacher using corporal punishment. Instead, they would go next door and ask a male teacher to administer the pain. I always found this odd. After all, if you've decided to hurt a small child, at least have the guts to do it yourself instead of using a proxy.

There was another form of punishment which was much worse than the physical ones—humiliation! Ah yes, there's nothing like a good dose of humiliation in front of your giggling peers to put you on the straight and narrow. Mr Selko, also known as "Psycho" was a master of humiliation. On rare occasions, he would take us for physical education when the sports teacher was off sick. He insisted the boys remove their underwear before putting their shorts on. (The same rule didn't apply to the girls regarding their underwear, probably because they wore skirts.) He was some sort of cleanliness nut-job and said that getting sweaty underpants was disgusting. He would take all the girls and boys outside, line the boys up against one wall, and the girls would line up opposite, with both genders were facing each other.

He'd slowly walk down the line of boys and slip his finger behind the elastic of our shorts, pull it back and peer down, checking we were not wearing any underwear (I know, weird right?) I remember the day one poor lad had either not heard the instructions correctly or wasn't aware of Psycho's tactics. The boy was made to take three paces forward, drop his shorts, and remove his underwear in front of a bunch of giggling girls. His face was understandably as red as a beetroot. Rest assured, if Psycho ever took us for PE, I made damn sure my jocks were resting safely back in the changing rooms.

I suppose the tactics teachers used in those days were similar to Pavlov's Dog theory. Whenever Pavlov fed his dog, he would constantly ring a bell. After a time, all he had to do was ring the bell and the dog would begin salivating. The dog had been conditioned to associate the sound of the bell with food. If you substitute the bell with physical or mental punishment, you have a similar situation—a deterrent.

This was the mid-seventies and the height of the baby boomers, so schools and classrooms were heaving under the weight of so many children. Forty-plus to a classroom was not unusual at my junior school, which probably had over five hundred kids attending. Punishment was employed to keep the pot from boiling over, and no one gave it a second thought. It was the norm. In fact, on the rare occasions, I got into trouble, I would try to hide it from my parents. If I had told them I had received the slipper or cane, they would have been incensed—not at the teachers—but at me!

I well remember my mother finding out about some minor indiscretion of mine, (talking in class) for which I'd received a hefty whack to the back of the knuckles on my left hand (always the left hand for right-handers, that way you could still hold a pen). As I explained my version of events, I recall her words vividly.

"Hmm, well, you must have been doing something wrong? Teachers don't hit you for nothing." When my father got home and my mother had grassed me up, he would gaze at me in a weary, disappointed way and say,

"Well lad, I hope you've learnt your bloody lesson?" I had friends whose parents weren't as easygoing as mine and they would receive another dose of corporal punishment. The teachers were never in the wrong!

Reading this back, it seems archaic, even barbaric, but as mentioned earlier—this was the norm; it was how things were done. If it makes my school days seem like hell on earth, it could not be further from the truth. My junior school days were some of the best days of my life and I look back on them fondly and still laugh at some of the events that took place.

Those days taught me some invaluable life lessons. The well-worn clichés of, "The school of hard knocks" and "The University of Life" hold some truth. I learnt to avoid psychos. Keep away from the "bad lads" who were always in trouble because you'd be tarred with the same brush. Circumnavigate the bullies; remove yourself completely from the manipulators and those who play mind games. Choose your friends carefully and lastly, always remove your underwear before performing any strenuous sporting activity, lest you be paraded naked down the high street.

For those of you who lived through those times, you will relate to some of this. For those of you who are younger, you will probably think it is far-fetched nonsense. I can assure you it's not far-fetched at all, it only deviates slightly from the truth. Well, my truth at least.

Chapter 6

Flasher Alert

The other day, I came across a new type of fiction called Flash Fiction. Apparently, it's all the rage (in a good sense). It's for people who are standing in queues (the British), and those who are doing short commutes (i.e. those on their way to jail or work—the same thing I guess.) These books (?) can be read in a few seconds.

Inspired, I wrote my own piece of Flash Fiction. I have reproduced it here for your delectation.

"Gone, In A Flash, Gordon" by Simon Northouse

Once upon a time, on a dark stormy night, everyone lived happily ever after. Apart from Gordon, who was "had up" for exposing himself in a public space often frequented by small furry animals and elderly ladies suffering from chronic lumbago.

The End.

The book is the first of a 5000 book series, tentatively titled, "The Curious Misadventures Of Gordon Flashman". I competitively priced each book at $10.99. I will create box sets containing a hundred books in each. These will have a page count of at least 10 and will be priced lower than buying the books individually. I like to give value for money. I aim to finish book 4999 by tomorrow night. Just in case anyone took this the wrong way—I'm joking, it's not £10.99, it's £9.99.

Chapter 7

In A Reverie

I used to assume the Latin phrase; "Tempus Fugit" was a swear term meaning "Please go away right now!" (I'm being polite.)

'Oi, Maximus, put that sword down; you'll have someone's bloody eye out! Now, tempus fugit!'

'Tempus fugit to you too, pal! Bloody Spartans! They think they run the joint!'

However, it actually means "Time Flies", and that is what this month's Mildly Interesting Fact is about.

Now, I'm no scientist but it doesn't stop me from thinking I am. I've been pondering the make-up of the universe lately, which makes a change from me pondering which colour socks I should wear each day.

There is something inherently wrong with how the universe works, in particular, how time works. Bear with me; I will not go deep here, mainly because I don't really have a clue what I'm talking about.

Have you noticed when you do boring tasks time slows down? When you sweep the yard, paint a fence, or watch an episode of Downton Abbey, the damn clock barely moves. Yet, the opposite is true when you are enjoying yourself. Having dinner with good friends, going on a long, beautiful walk with your family, or watching re-runs on YouTube of politicians falling down steps, then the clock spins by at an exponential rate.

Thanks to my capability for intensive and exhaustive research (yep, Google again), I found out scientists have studied this phenomenon. You'd think they'd have more important matters to be studying such as a cure for Ebola, finding an emissions-free power source or figuring out why the only thing cling film clings to, is itself—but I digress. It appears the old saying, "time flies when you're having fun" has some truth to it.

Time Perception is the phrase used to describe these events, and it is a trick of the brain. When our minds are fully engaged on something, we are not aware of time. On the other hand, when we are listening to upper management talk about increasing stakeholder synergy within a seamless integrated vertical platform, we perceive that time has slowed down or, in my case, going backwards. Why? Because we are now acutely aware of time. We look at our watches or the clock on the wall and think, "I must change jobs", "My God, this guy is a boring tit", or "I really must check my tyre pressure on the way home".

Some of you will be wondering why I brought this subject up. Others will be looking at their watches thinking, "Yep, he's right, time has definitely slowed down. I could swear I've been reading this rubbish for at least two hours, but in fact, it's only twenty seconds."

A few weeks ago I woke up in the morning (duh!), lay in bed, and recalled an event that happened to me over thirty years ago. I went to a nightclub and met a girl. This girl was the most beautiful creature on the planet... *disclaimer*: until I met my future wife, of course. (W*atch it Northouse, you're on shaky ground*—Ed). She was super posh (the mystery girl, not the missus) and her father was a prominent politician at the time. Her family was rich, powerful, and privileged. I, on the other hand, was an apprentice bricklayer and all-round shit-kicker from a rough part of Leeds. We had absolutely nothing in common and at first, she wouldn't even give me the time of day. However, being a persistent young chap and a randy bugger, to boot, I kept chipping away until her facade finally cracked. We talked for hours and there was a chemistry between us. I finally left, alone, and our paths never crossed again. Not once, in the intervening years, has my mind thought about her, until a few weeks back.

Why, after all this time, would that memory resurface? I idly wondered what might have happened had we started a relationship. Within minutes, I was up and away and my next book was being played out like a film in my head. For the following two days, I was in a complete reverie.

I hung a basket of dirty washing out on the line, brought a clean batch in, and put it in the washing machine. I fed the dog cat food and the cat dog food. The dog didn't give a toss; in fact, she seemed to enjoy the change. The cat, however, is still sulking with me to this day. I put sugar in my tea, which I haven't done for twenty years. I forgot to pick my daughter up from netball training. I called my wife, Alan, on at least two occasions, at one point completely forgot the names of my daughters and referred to them as "thingamabob" and "whatshername" for a few hours. One day, I was parked outside the supermarket wondering why my car door wouldn't open. The answer soon became obvious—it wasn't my car—it wasn't even the same model or colour!

Those two days felt like a few brief hours—my mind was completely absorbed with my story and nothing else.

All the females in my life are great at multi-tasking. They can bake bread, fill out their child's excursion form, talk to their friend on the phone, repaint the bathroom ceiling, and memorise all the lyrics to Adele's "Someone Like You", all at the same time, without missing a beat. Their brains are like multiple ring-roads with never-ending forks and side routes, all interweaving and overlapping.

Most of the men I know cannot multi-task. On the odd occasions I've tried to, it ends up a right bloody shambles! I once tried to reconcile my bank statement whilst holding a conversation with my wife and writing a letter to my mother. My wife gave up on the conversation within seconds as she said I was speaking a newly invented language called "utter crap". My mother received a stiff missive from me ranting about bank fees and my bank manager got a very moving letter from me telling him how much I missed and loved him and how was the cat and Mrs Brown's lumbago. Most disturbingly, I received a response from him asking me if I was available for drinks on Friday night followed by a candlelit dinner. Oh, and don't forget to bring my overnight bag!

Men's brains only have one road. It's a six-lane superhighway that travels from the frontal lobe right to the back cortex. Traffic can only flow in one direction and there are no turnoffs or slip-roads. Three of the lanes are reserved specifically for sexual thoughts, two lanes for sport and food, and the last lane for everything else. It's always been a mystery to me that most of the powerful institutions in the world and big business are run by men —no wonder the world is stuffed! Give the job to a handful of multi-tasking women and we'd have peace, love, and prosperity for all, overnight. Anyway, I digress slightly—back to my reverie.

I sat down and began to write. I had everything in my head and needed to get it down on paper as quickly as possible. I figured I had one full-length novel of between 80 to 100k words and a prequel novella of about 30k words. After four days, I had 28k words and had hardly begun to scratch the surface. I realised I needed to do some planning, something I rarely do when writing. I got a large A2 sized art pad and drew a circle on it. For each chapter, I drew a line extending away from the edge of the circle and wrote a brief sentence describing the scene and the characters in it. After thirty minutes, I was done. There were now three full-length novels sketched out.

I'd begin writing at 9 am and would take a break after a couple of hours, but it wasn't two hours that had passed, it was four or five hours. Time had flown. I'd break off about 6 pm to make dinner for Alan, "whatshername" and "thingamabob" and once dinner was done, I was back to the keyboard.

The story is about the young couple who met in that nightclub all those years ago. It is set in 1984, just before the start of the miners' strike (for those of you who are unaware, the miners' strike of '84 were one of the most divisive periods in modern British history). It's a lot more serious than my previous books, (although there are still plenty of laughs going on). It is set to a backdrop of political unrest, mistrust, a young man trying to make his mark on the world and a band of close-knit friends. However, primarily it is a love story. It's even got a few sex scenes in it. These are not there for crass titillation, as having read them back, there is very little titillating going on. They are not graphic, or pornographic, things are sort of alluded to rather than described in detail. The purpose of them is to show the intensity and passion of the relationship.

This is not a lovey-dovey, rosy coloured romance that ends with everyone living happily ever after. It is raw, passionate, pulsating, and realistic. It reminds me of those classic black and white films from the early sixties, which were based on novels by the "Angry Young Man" brigade. Films like "Saturday Night Sunday Morning", "A Room At The Top", "Billy Liar" and "A Kind Of Loving" to name but a few. Don't get me wrong, it is not bleak. In fact, it is quite heart-warming really, and it clicks along at a good pace.

As mentioned earlier, I was born and raised in Yorkshire. Now, the Yorkshire folk can be called many things, and often are, but we are not the most emotive people in the world. The only time a man may shed a tear is when his football team loses or someone knocks his pint over. Our women folk only cry when one of their favourite characters from a soap opera is killed off. Okay, that's not quite true—but you get my drift.

However, writing the book has had me choking up occasionally (come on, I'm not going to admit I cry). Maybe I've found finally found my feminine side. Then in the next chapter, I would laugh like a drain. I know it is not good protocol to laugh at one's own jokes, but reading the words back, it was as if someone else had written them.

The most disturbing thing is I've fallen head-over-heels in love with the protagonist's girlfriend! It's insane, but I cannot stop thinking about her. I know the colour of her hair, her eyes, the way she talks, the way she moves, her funny little sayings—I am besotted with the girl. When my wife asks me how the book is coming along, I get all defensive and secretive.

"Why? What are you implying, don't you trust me? There's absolutely nothing going on. Check my phone if you like." She gazes at me, sadly, as though I'm bonkers. How can a man fall in love with a figment of his own imagination? It's unhealthy, unwise, and bloody unhelpful! I may need therapy after I finish the last book.

For me, it feels like only a couple of days ago since I finished my last newsletter and hit the send button, but it is, in fact, 23 days ago. The next few months are going to fly by and soon I will be sporting 3-inch-long fingernails and nasal hair dangling over my top lip.

So, back to my original point about there being something wrong with the universe. Wouldn't you think the laws of nature or even our own brains would have turned things the opposite way around? Instead of it feeling like it takes three hours to unpack the shopping and unclog the drain, it should whizz by in seconds. The beautiful family day spent at the beach, which flew by in less than an hour, should seem like twenty hours. The dull should go fast and the enjoyable should go slow. If it did, I would have finished my three books by now. Maybe when the universe finally stops expanding and begins to contract, things will reverse, and the good times will seem to last forever, and the bad days will vanish in seconds. It's a nice dream to have.

Chapter 8

Work... What Is It Good For?

W ork, what is it good for? Good God, y'all! Don't say, absolutely nothing!

Of course, work is good for something. Money, for one thing, and for getting things done. Without work, there would be no society. However, I must be honest with you; I spent more years than I care to recollect working for a multinational company as a technical writer. I can say, without doubt, this was the most boring time of my life. I know you think life in the Northouse homestead would be one big roller coaster ride of laughs, witty asides, humorous anecdotes, and mindless good humour. Well, you'd be right, that's exactly what it's like when I'm not home, but sometimes we all have to do boring things. Boring things bore me, oddly enough, and I try to put the boring stuff off for as long as possible. Where am I going with this? I really have no idea. (*Surprise, surprise—Ed*).

This brings me neatly onto the word "manager"

"Hang on, how did he extrapolate manager from that?"

Keep up, you at the back. Work / boring things /manager—you see the connection? No? Okay, well don't worry, it's all explained in this month's mildly interesting fact.

When I worked at the multinational company for excruciatingly dull things, I remember a discussion I had with one of my female colleagues. She had taken exception to the word "manager," unlike me, who had taken exception to the "actual" manager. She believed the word was sexist and the title "manager" should be renamed as People and Workflow Coordinator. I know, pretty snappy, eh?

I like words, the sound of them, the look of them on paper and some words make me all happy inside. Words like flabbergasted, discombobulated, Hessian, flibbertigibbet, contumely, and brake fluid. You're thinking the last one is odd, right? It's a contradiction in terms. Brake—meaning to stop and fluid for motion. Amazing!

When my colleague complained about the word, "manager" I decided to do some research (yes, I'm odd). Unfortunately, Google did not exist in those days so I had to use something the young 'uns will never have heard of; Netscape Navigator, which was a bit like Google on elephant tranquillisers.

My colleague wrongly assumed the man in manager referred to the male of the human species and was therefore sexist. However, it has nothing to do with men, or man, or males. Manager derives from the Latin word "manus" *(always with the Latin—Ed)*. It means "hand" and the Italian word "maneggiare" means to control. So, a manager is a hand controller, which sounds a bit dodgy, but Latin is a strange language.

During my time at Purgatory Inc, there were three things I despised: meetings, team-bonding days and the Christmas party. In fact, I actually developed a phobia of meetings but there was no Latin medical term for the condition, so I had to invent my own.

'Jerkocircophobia' (@Simon Northouse, 1999) means a morbid and irrational fear of meetings.

There are a finite number of hours in everyone's lives and wasting those precious hours listening to Kevin from OH&S waffle on about the dangers of lacerating your jugular vein with a paper cut or impaling oneself on a hole punch can seem rather inconsequential.

I'm quite proud of the word "Jerkocircophobia" and please, feel free to use it—there's no charge. In fact, bear with me; I'm going to Google it to make sure it has not been coined by anyone else. Nope, all good, there's plenty of things about jerk circles, whatever they are, but definitely no 'Jerkocircophobia.'

Now, don't misunderstand me, I'm not against meetings per se. Philosophically, I can appreciate their importance. In fact, while I've been in meetings, I've often used the time to ponder how, why and when meetings first entered the human psyche. They were obviously once important.

I can well understand the elders of the tribe getting together every Monday morning to discuss vexing issues that faced their clan. A meeting would be very handy should someone catch wind the neighbouring village of cannibals are planning a surprise attack during the tribe's weekly bath night. Concerns could be aired, plans could be made, delegation of authority could be handed down, minutes taken, and fears allayed. Likewise, if a rogue sabre-toothed tiger was on the prowl, gobbling up little children and the hard of hearing, a meeting would be beneficial to decide how to deal with the errant feline.

Meetings may have been convened for more mundane matters, such as, "Please, could the Attack and Pillage Committee remind their team members to carry their spears upright at all times when not in battle. Last week, we had three near-miss incidents, which could have resulted in a blinding, a partial circumcision, and an unnecessary colonoscopy."

Alas, the modern meeting is very different. Why? Because they are mainly a waste of your time, a stage for those with nothing to say to hold court. The problem with any group gathering which encourages the attendees to air their views and ideas is that, unfortunately, they invariably do. I'm not sure whether meetings are the same the world over (and I suspect they are) but the meetings I had the misfortune to attend were populated with half-wits, the clinically insane, pathological egocentrics, narcissists, the hard of understanding, the proactively disenfranchised,

Dodgy Dave and worst of all, middle management. I include myself in the list—guess which one I was?

Not once in the thousands of meetings I attended over the years did a meeting begin on time. Not only that, but I could count on the fingers of a one-fingered hand how many times I left a meeting and thought to myself, "Hmm, that was productive."

I had nothing against getting together with a few colleagues during the week to discuss some pressing issues like why are so many people spelling the word "specific" as "pacific"? Or why do people insist on capitalising common nouns? I know, riveting, right?

One day, I received an email from my manager stating all meetings were now mandatory to attend. I don't know about you, but I hate being told what to do. It's an anti-authority thing I've had since I was a child. Don't worry, I'm not a homicidal maniac—honest.

I spoke earlier about words I love. I also have a list of words I hate, such as; vagary, ballcock, cloche, Switzerland, clamp, hither and mandatory—to name but a few. From that day on, I never attended another meeting. People worried for me, "You must attend, it's mandatory." No, it's not bloody mandatory! It's mandatory I keep to the speed limit. It's mandatory I pay my income tax. It's mandatory I don't drive when I'm over the limit and it's mandatory I remove my toenail clippings from the bathroom sink when I've finished! However, it is not mandatory I attend a pointless meeting!

From that day on, I never attended another meeting, and guess what? The world kept turning. My productivity soared, which in turn made my manager look good, so he turned a blind eye to me not attending his mandatory meetings (that were not mandatory).

I have a very simple outlook to work. It is a business contract between an employer and an employee or contractor. As an employee, I do the work the employer wants me to do, and they pay me for the hours I work. I give my time—they give me money in return. If, after a month, they realise I am good at my job, they keep giving me more work and they keep paying me. They're happy and I'm unhappy, but at least I'm paying the bills and putting food on the table for my family. It is a simple and easily understood coalition.

If, after a month, they realise I'm totally feckless and incompetent at my job—then the solution is simple—they promote me to a managerial role in another department and are rid of me. This is how it used to work. But things changed in the nineties—and I blame the Americans! (*Watch it boyo, most of your readers are from LaLaLand—Ed.*)

In the nineties, the world was inundated with feel-good, self-help, time management, leadership, and how to get-rich-quick books written by white-middle-aged-American men. I am actually embarrassed to admit I read a few of those books.

They were always the same. They sold the idea you could be whatever you wanted to be by simply visualising it. Sorry, but that is complete codswallop! (Another noble word.) Visualising something in your head does not make it happen. If it did, I would have spent many a long and happy night with Nicole Kidman, Demi Moore, and Angela Lansbury in a dungeon (don't ask, it's complicated).

Thought must be married with action to achieve anything. There is a time for thinking and a time for doing, and I do not need a guy whose smile could blind you from a thousand paces to tell me that.

Which brings me back to meetings, "It does?" Yes, it does. Please keep up!

The failure of most meetings is they are people's thought bubbles. Thoughts are spoken, and that's it. There is rarely any doable action to be undertaken after the thought bubble has passed. Meetings are the refuge of those who do not have enough work to do; of those who like the sound of their own voice, and of those who like to feel important even though they realise they're not. So, my advice would be, if you want to achieve something, think about it, then put those thoughts into action, and keep away from bloody meetings, they'll suck the life out of you!

If you can feel my antipathy towards meetings, then wait until the next newsletter when I smite down the biggest waste of time of any workplace activity—Team-Bonding. Even the words send me into a cold sweat.

Next month I will recount the one and only time I attended a team-bonding day. It was about as enjoyable as my visit to a proctologist with fingers the size of cucumbers and a poor sense of humour! Never a good mix, in my humble opinion.

Chapter 9

Team-Bonding

I 've been busy this last month putting the finishing touches to the third book in the Shooting Star series, Fall Of A Shooting Star. It was 80% complete about six months ago, but the last 20% has been a real ball-ache. There were a few plot holes that needed tidying up. The trouble is, when writing, once you change something after the event, it has a knock-on effect throughout the entire book. It's like throwing a pebble into a pond and seeing the ripples expand forever outwards.

I did what any talented writer would do *(presumption, my friend, presumption—Ed)* and I avoided it. After all, a problem ignored is a problem solved. At one stage it got so bad I tackled all the other problems I've been avoiding, to avoid finishing the book. I cleaned my office, removed leaves from the gutters, cut the grass even though there's nothing to cut. I even got into a long conversation with the bloke on duty at the council tip, something I'd vowed never to do again after my last harrowing experience. He's a nice enough chap, but he's had a personality transplant and he makes watching grass grow seem like an extreme sport.

However, I finally knuckled down and am now racing towards the finishing line at the speed of a glacier. Okay, let's get on with it *(my thoughts exactly—Ed.)*

Oxytocin? Does anyone know what it is? (Okay, well done you over there. There's always a smartarse lurking in the background). I'll be honest with you; I had no idea what it was until I stumbled upon some interesting research into team-bonding (I told you I've been avoiding finishing my book).

To me, oxytocin sounds like one of those high-fibre bedtime drinks for people with a sluggish bowel. However, it's not. It is actually a chemical released by the brain during sexual orgasm *(is there any other type of orgasm—Ed.)* Research conducted by IPRAFT (Institute of Pointless Research Again Funded by the Taxpayer) found this same chemical is released during team-bonding days. *WTF! GET OUT OF HERE!* I kid you not.

I'm not exactly sure what team-bonding games were being played at the time the research was being conducted, but it certainly didn't reflect my team-bonding experiences. I can honestly state, with hand on heart, there was no oxytocin released from my brain during our team-building days. Melatonin, yes, but oxytocin, no.

Bigas Vinculum is Latin for team-bonding. I know it sounds like a vulgar term for a certain part of the female anatomy, but that's Latin for you. Now, I'm no scholar, *(really? I wouldn't have guessed—Ed)* but I'm pretty sure the Romans didn't take part in many meetings or team-bonding sessions, otherwise, they'd never have moved further than the walls of Rome. Although, I suppose ransacking and pillaging is a form of team-bonding if you're into that sort of caper. The Romans were action men (and women). They'd look at a map of Europe or North Africa and say, 'Yep, we'll have Gaul this week and next month I fancy a holiday in Crete. Let's do it!'

As middle and upper management are wont to do, one year during my stint at Purgatory Inc, they thought it would be a splendid idea to send our department on a Bigas Vinculum day.

Come the big day, a coach drove our group of eighteen to the Stalag, where we began our bonding session. The first thing our team-bonding "mentor" did was to split us up into six teams of three. I did bring to the mentor's attention that splitting the group up was the opposite of what team-bonding was about. I could tell from the hatred in his eyes he saw me as a troublemaker—too bloody right!

For sins from a previous life, I was grouped with Hypochondriac Harry and Numerical Norman. Harry was a decent bloke but his drain on the health system was greater than the GDP of some third-world countries. I have empathy. I have sympathy. I am not immune to the suffering of my fellow man or woman. But, when you've listened to Harry for fifteen minutes each day of your working life, describe his ailments to you, then... well, your empathy diminishes somewhat. To listen about the inner workings (or outer) of his irritable bowel first thing on a Monday morning is not the best start to a week. I'd have been irritable if I'd been Harry's bowel.

As for Numerical Norman, he was head of accounts. He was a dull-witted chap who suffered from halitosis, rampaging dandruff, and worst of all, an appalling dress sense. I'm sure his grandmother dressed him each day. I'm unsure if there's a word for it, but he had the equivalent of numerical dyslexia. I found this out after my first month on the job when I checked my bank balance. To my immense pleasure, I noticed I'd been paid £120'000 for a month's work. I was bloody good at my job, and to be honest, worth every cent, but something told me there had been a foul-up in accounts. The foul-up was Norman, one of many foul-ups. Of course, I ended up paying the money back, begrudgingly.

The following month, I received no payment at all. After two weeks of investigation, it was revealed my wage had gone to a Mr Unbutoo in Nigeria, for which I am sure he was eternally grateful. He withdrew all the money, closed his bank account and was last seen in a drunken stupor, stumbling around the streets of Abuja singing "Girls Just Wanna Have Fun" by Cyndi Lauper. With the power of hindsight, I wish I had done the same (apart from the choice of song). Anyway, I digress. Back to team-bonding.

Our glorious "mentor" set us all our first team-bonding task. He placed in front of us a plastic straw, a paper clip, a rubber band and asked us to construct a replica of the Eiffel Tower. Apparently, it took ten minutes of CPR, a dozen zaps from a defibrillator, a good whiff of Mrs Bandy's Miraculous Sniffing Salts and a dose of Dr Gripes Nerve Syrup to bring me around. When I finally resumed my seat, I set to the task with gusto. Harry and Norman were about as much use as tits on a bull, so I knew I'd have to sail the ship alone. We'd been allocated ten minutes to complete the task. After thirty seconds, I was done and informed the mentor. He studied my masterpiece for a few nanoseconds and didn't look impressed. Granted, to the naked eye, it may have looked like a plastic straw with a paper clip attached to it with the aid of a rubber band. However, as I explained to him, he was looking at it through a physical prism. He needed to view it through the metaphysical eye. After all, art is subjective. We came last.

I'm not sure what unfolded for the next two hours because I said I had an urgent dental appointment and escaped. In fact, having a root canal would have been preferable to spending another minute in the team-bonding Gulag.

I returned at 2 pm, hoping the day was all but over. What a naïve, foolish innocent abroad I was. As we all trooped onto the coach, our mentor informed us we were all about to have some "great fun". His words sent a shiver down my spine. He informed us we were heading to the Croquet Club. I desperately ransacked my lunchbox looking for my cyanide pills. Alas, my dear wife had forgotten to pack them that particular day. Numerical Norman idly informed me his mother was good at knitting. I was grateful for this piece of information and will now die a happy man.

For those lucky few who don't know what croquet is, I'll explain. British toffs invented croquet to pass the time away. When they weren't busy invading other countries, shooting peasants, or groping their housemaids, they needed something to occupy their minds. Being well educated, to the manor-born and naturally ingenious, they put their collective heads together and came up with the game of croquet.

It basically involves bending a coat hanger into a "U" shape and sticking it into the ground. A ball, about three inches in diameter, is then whacked through the hoops with a mallet you've borrowed from your gardener. There are no points and no rules, and no one wins or loses. The game ends when news comes through that there's a peasant shoot beginning on Lord Dingletwat's estate at 3 pm—prompt. At this point, the game is abandoned, and everyone tucks into cucumber sandwiches, iced tea, and a good serving of Eton Mess. After high tea, the lady folk retire to their embroidery room to knit teapots and the men don their shooting jackets and get their butler to piggyback them to Lord Dingletwat's estate, twelve miles away.

Thankfully, our game of croquet came to an abrupt, and disturbing halt when Hypochondriac Harry had a giddy turn while attempting to extricate his mallet from an elderly lady who had been bent over doing a spot of weeding nearby. He was lucky to escape being put on the sex-offenders register.

At the start of the day, we had been a bunch of co-workers, tolerant and accepting of each other's strengths and weaknesses. By the end of the day, we were six disparate teams of three. Hating, sniping, and vowing revenge on each other for the rest of eternity. Hmm, team-bonding, indeed.

Chapter 10

Genre, Genre, Genre

Have you ever had one of those months where you say to yourself, "What a hell of a month!"

Well, that's been my month. There's been the good, the bad, and the fugly.

I've attended a wedding, been on a long road trip with my family, had the clutch go in my car, had the gearbox go in my wife's car, spent a night in gaol, had the air-con for the house give up the ghost, suffered from a swollen finger and found a foreign body in my pasta.

"Hang on a mo!" I can hear you cry, "back-up a bit... you spent a night where?" Yes, in gaol. I found it quite pleasant, although the rest of the family were less than impressed, as we did all have to share a cell together.

Family holidays are always stressful. As I explained to my kids, family getaways are not meant to be enjoyed at the time they happen. No, it's only upon returning home, unpacking, and allowing a few days to pass, before we can all look back fondly on our time together. By then we have forgotten about the bitch-fights in the car, the spiders, and rats in the gaol cell, the short-curly hair loitering with malevolent intent in my linguine, and the slack-jawed moron who nearly ran us off the road. Ah, great times.

Anyway, enough twaddle; let us move on to this month's Mildly Interesting Fact. I'm a writer, (stop sniggering), so I deal with words. I like to know their meaning *(always helpful... being a writer—Ed)* and I like to investigate their origin and how they evolved. Therefore, this month, I'm looking at the word "Genre" and for good reason, although that reason may not be obvious at first, or even ever.

Genre is a French word, meaning "sort, style, kind" and is related to the word "gender". But as with most things, everything comes back to Latin. The French language was based on Latin. Okay, that sounds low brow. The French people didn't wake up one day and say, "Hey, Pierre, I have a great idea, why don't we invent a new language based on Latin? We'll call it French!" No, language evolves over time.

Latin was the official language of the Romans, and as we know, the Romans liked to get about a bit. Think of them as the Russian tourists of today, but not as aggressive. The Romans loved Europe, North Africa, and the Middle East. In fact, they liked it so much they kept it, well, for a time at least. They went as far north as northern England then stopped, which was odd, as the Romans weren't the stopping type. However, on reflection, if you've ever spent a winter in Scotland (or a summer) you'd understand why—however—I digress.

The French word Genre can be traced back to the Latin word Genus (there is no "I" in Genus) and Genus means birth, race, kind, and sort. In short, it's a classification word.

As an aside, if you left the letter "E" out of Genus you'd have a herd of wildebeest rampaging through your newsletter right now *(you're digressing again—get on with it! Ed)*

Okay, so what is the point of all this? *(Good question—Ed.)* Well, it's all about genre, something which is very important to a writer. It's the equivalent of location, location, location, to a real estate agent.

For the few who haven't already hit the unsubscribe button with a certain amount of zeal, read on.

Books are classified into genres, and I often ask myself what "genre" I write in. I have four completely different series published at the moment.

The Shooting Star series, Soul Love series, The School Days series and this twaddle I'm writing now—The Discombobulated Newsletter series.

None of them are easy to classify as they are not written to market. They are not mystery although there is some mystery in the first two series. They are not romance, but there is romance in the Soul Love series along with a bit of paranormal. There are varying amounts of humour (or attempts at humour) in all the books, but humour is not a standalone genre. It makes them damned hard to market, and I always end dumping them in the satire/parody/comedy categories on Amazon.

It would be nice if the powers-that-be invented a new genre called, "A bit of everything," or "Omni-genre." When asked, "what genre are you?" I could confidently reply, "Omni-genre."

Parody is used as a device to imitate and mock someone or something. It is designed to make one laugh or at least smile. Satire is slightly different. It uses humour mixed with varying degrees of anger or frustration to make a point. Great parody should make you laugh. Great satire should make you think. Satire is a great tool for a writer as it gives us a chance to let a character show their true colours without the author bludgeoning the reader with a statement of fact. I'll give a quick example from a new book that I'm writing at the moment.

The character, Joe, is in his late fifties and basically, he's sexist against women. He is not a misogynist, he does not hate women, but deep down he believes in the old-fashioned values of men being in charge. However, he would never admit to this, as he wants to be seen as a reasonable and modern thinking man. In my book, I could have simply said, "It was plain to see that Joe was sexist, despite his protestations." That's okay, it makes its point, and the reader is left in no doubt about Joe. However, instead, I used a bit of satire to weave more colour into the paragraph and to let Joe show us he is sexist. The excerpt below involves a conversation between Joe and the protagonist, Jimmy (who is aged twenty).

"I believe women, girls, should be treated exactly like men. They should have the same opportunities that are available to men. Unfortunately, there is a lot of ingrained sexism in our society," said Jimmy with a fire in his belly. Joe sat down in his special chair and stared at Jimmy for a moment.

"Quite right, young man. I couldn't agree more," Joe replied thoughtfully. "Darling?" he called out to his wife. "Did you iron my white shirt yet? I am due at the club in an hour. Oh, and while you're in the kitchen, would you put the kettle on and make me a cup of tea, there's a dear."

This brief excerpt tells us way more about Joe than the first, matter-of-fact statement. We know Joe has a chair, his chair that no one else is presumably allowed to sit in. Joe is King, the chair, his throne. He's incapable of ironing his own shirt as he doesn't know how to—he's never done it before. His wife is in the kitchen, apparently in her domain. He asks for a cup of tea. He doesn't offer to make a cup of tea for Jimmy or his wife. He's also rather patronising, referring to Jimmy as "young man", and using the phrase "there's a dear" to his wife. Now, that paragraph is more "wry" than funny, but by using satire, Joe has shown us his true colours.

There are many phrases in the English language that describe someone who brings about their own downfall. One of my favourites was used by Shakespeare, "hoist with his own petard". A petard is an old word for a small bomb. Hoist means to go up. Therefore, blown up by one's own bomb. The phrase these days is used to mean brought down by one's own words or deeds.

Satire doesn't have to be laugh-out-loud funny. In fact, I find the best satire is the type that makes me smile and wince at the same time. When this happens, I know the writer has hit the nail on the head.

Chapter 11

Misinterpretation

As I write this, it is exactly 50 years ago today since one of the greatest moments in the history of humanity (and womankind) occurred. Yes, you guessed it, "Give Peace A Chance" by John Lennon and the Plastic Ono Band, peaked at number 2 in the UK singles charts, a travesty of justice as it should have hit the top spot.

For any millennials who are a bit bamboozled by the above statement, let me explain. A "single" was a round piece of vinyl, 7 inches in diameter that was placed on a machine called a record player. The single spun around and when a needle was placed on top of it, music came out of a speaker. Furthermore, you had to walk to a record shop and purchase a record with money if you wanted to listen to music. I know, it sounds archaic and ridiculous, doesn't it? Wait, stop: I'm being facetious, fatuous, frivolous.

This is the problem with the written word. It is easy for the reader to misinterpret the author's true intent. For all of you familiar with my monthly ramblings, you know this newsletter is a bit of fun, tongue-in-cheek, irreverent, and as one person informed me, "bloody long-winded." This same person also told me they didn't have time to read because they were too busy. I understand, I really do. This email is not intended to be read when you're frantically strapping the kids into the car, mowing the lawn or de-sexing your neighbour's ferrets. It is to be perused at leisure, during a coffee break or in the office when you're supposed to be working. People can stop and start at will or choose not to read it at all.

Last month I received an email from a person who wasn't just angry, they were bloody livid! They said they had never signed up for the newsletter and my jokes were lame, and as payback for this infringement of liberty, they were going to sock it to me, by unsubscribing. I know my jokes are lame; some of them should be on life support. As for not signing up for my newsletter, that is a different kettle of turnips. Everyone must go through the process of signing up for it, either on a book promo site or from my website. There is no other way I could know your email address.

I wondered why the person in question, didn't simply hit unsubscribe and be done with it. They felt the need to give me a "bloody nose" as they exited, which is fine. Better to have a go at me than kick the cat. All of this brings me neatly on to this month's Mildly Interesting Fact.

Ira Illud, (as text-rage is called in Latin) is a modern-day phenomenon. Apparently, it is most common when dealing with emails. People who have a short fuse and expect their modern-day communications to be concise and snappy can get bloody annoyed when confronted with a communique that is longer than a telephone number. Also, because the email is a one-way street, i.e. only the sender is talking, people can feel disempowered.

Not only that, but it is easy to misinterpret the sender's true intent. The reader may think they are being patronised or insulted. They may regard the email as hostile or passive-aggressive because there is no one-on-one communication. When we talk face to face with someone, we can tell by the tone of their voice or facial expressions what their true intent is. In fact, in situations like these, words are almost secondary, as we pick up cues from body language. There's now a whole lexicon of words that have "rage" as a suffix or a prefix.

Page-rage: I'll put my hand up to this one. I suffer from this all the time. The official description is of someone who leaves nasty reviews on social media or websites. I don't do that, but I do suffer from an offshoot of page-rage. You know when you're reading a terrible book, *(I'm sure your readers know exactly what you mean—Ed)* but you persist with it night after night in the hope it will get better... and it doesn't. Then one night, after a particularly atrocious split-infinitive, followed immediately by a dangling modifier, you launch the book at the wall. Yes, there's many a famous author who has face-planted into my plasterboard.

Rage-clean: Bit of a misnomer, this one. It doesn't mean to clean up in a state of extreme anger. It takes "rage" as an informal verb. It means to clean quickly. The type of cleaning you do when your wife has been hard at work all day and you've been binge watching "The Walking Dead" on Netflix while digesting ten packets of Cheezels. You look around the house and realise it's a bombsite. You notice the clock and say, "Blood and thunder! My sweetness and light will be home in ten minutes. Time for a rage-clean."

You run around like a headless chicken, throwing anything not nailed down into the shoe cupboard. You vac the floor, polish the cat, and start the dishwasher—even though there's nothing in it. Finally, you pull all the curtains shut and lower the lighting just in time. When she asks what I've been up to all day, I reply, with exhausted weariness,

"Haven't bloody stopped cleaning all day, love. I'm worn out." Oh, yes, I've been there many times. In fact, I'll be doing a rage-clean as soon as I've finished this newsletter.

Rage-buy: It happens all the time. Those instances when you are forced to buy something imperative to your well-being. It could be a new set of tyres for your car. A replacement air-conditioner before the onset of a blisteringly hot summer, or a three pack of Calvin Klein underpants. You don't want to buy them, but you must. To rub salt into the wound, the article in question is so expensive it gives you a nosebleed. You know you are being shafted but there's nothing you can do about it because it is an essential item. So begins rage-buy. You deliberately pick a fight with the shop assistant, scream, "What are you staring at?" to a small child, then jump in the car, shaking with rage-buy which quickly morphs into road-rage.

Whine-rage: My daughters, and occasionally my wife, suffer from this condition, *(ooh, you're a brave man, Northouse... or stupid—Ed)*. When I pick my girls up after work or a school excursion, I am the recipient of whine-rage. My God, they can carry on! You'd assume they were living in a third-world country, wearing rags, and ravished with hunger. The weather's too hot or too cold, the school trip was boring, they didn't enjoy the caramel flambé in their lunchbox; they weren't allowed their smartphones on the coach. If there were a world championship for never-ending whining, my two would be serious contenders. When they're both in the car at the same time, I get stereophonic whingeing. It's at times like these I visit my special place, deep inside my head.

Rage-cancel: This occurs when you are purchasing something online. For reasons best known to itself, the transaction is taking longer than expected. At 5 seconds you become annoyed. After 10 seconds you are seething and after 20 seconds you are in a sweaty, uncontrollable rage. Your only recourse for this injustice? To cancel the order. Welcome to rage-cancel.

Rage-decorating: This is something I have been guilty of in the past. When we are expecting visitors coming to stay with us, my wife suddenly becomes all house-proud. It doesn't seem to bother her we live in squalor for the other 51 weeks of the year. She gives me a list of jobs to do. Repaint the front room, fix the back door, stain the deck, weed the garden and bitumen the bathroom ceiling, oh, and don't forget to fix the hole in the plasterboard you made when you threw Jeffrey Archer at it the other night. I complete my chores with gritted teeth raging inside.

Queue-rage: Being British, I never suffer queue-rage. As you know, the Brits invented queuing as a way to pass the time of day until something more interesting came along. We queue in silence, well aware of the grand order of things. Without orderly queuing, what have you got? Chaos, that's what! As my next-door neighbour, René Descartes, once said, "I queue, therefore I am." A bit of a thinker is old René, although he's not the sort of person you'd invite to a party to liven things up. To the Brits, the most heinous crime you can commit is to queue jump. There's a special place in hell for those types.

Air-rage: I'm sure most people have at least witnessed this. There's nothing worse... well, apart from queue jumpers, of course. There's always some cock-muppet who has to have a pop at the air hostess. He may well be a vegetarian with a violent allergic reaction to peanuts, but there's no need to go off like a pork chop because he's been served skewered satay chicken for lunch. Suck it up, big boy, and move on. Of course, this is actually a combination of air-rage and food-rage.

Food-rage: You've seen him, I've seen him—the guy in the restaurant who wants to draw attention to himself, because of feelings of inadequacy. Now he plans to stuff up everyone's evening by acting like a baby who hasn't slept for 24 hours and is teething. There's always something wrong with the meal. The meat's too rare or it's overdone. The ice cream isn't cold enough, the coffee is not the correct shade of black, the water's too wet. Even if a trio of 3-star, Michelin chefs, made up of Marco Pierre White, Gordon Ramsay, and Kanye West, served up a plate of Japanese Wagyu steak with truffle sauce, infused with saffron, this guy would complain the decor was not to his liking. Talking of Kanye West, for years I assumed it was Aldi's home-brand tuna until my daughter enlightened me.

Actually, you may find this hard to believe, but I was once the instigator of a food-rage incident, *(strangely, I can believe it—Ed.)* A couple of years ago I went out for a meal with my wife and daughters to a fancy-schmancy, super expensive restaurant *(obviously before you were trying to make a living as an author—Ed.)* Can you please shut up! I'm trying to write here!

I ordered oysters for my starter. They arrived with the obligatory lemon quarters to squeeze over them. As I gripped the lemon slice, it suddenly flew from my grip at the speed of a bullet. It shot across the restaurant and hit an elderly gentleman in the neck as he was tucking into his dessert of "distressed peach melba". Don't ask me why his peach melba was distressed. Maybe it had been handed a speeding ticket earlier in the day, or perhaps its partner had desserted them *(oh, dear ... Ed)* but I digress.

The elderly man was less than impressed at being hit in the throat by a piece of citrus. He immediately accused the party sat opposite him of launching the fruit cruise missile. A hell of a ruckus erupted, which quickly spread like wildfire throughout the dining room. Meanwhile, I slurped on my oysters, watching the free entertainment. A fun night was had by all, well, by me at least. Boy, did those oysters taste good, although a tad more lemon juice wouldn't have gone amiss.

Alas, that is the end of this rage-athon. I'm sure as we saunter through the years, more rage suffixes and prefixes will appear. I can already hear a smartphone hitting the wall as someone flies into a newsletter-rage.

Chapter 12

Getting To The Bottom Of Things

A couple of years ago, I had something peculiar going on downstairs. No, I'm not talking about weird noises coming from the cellar. I'm trying to be polite and tactful. Let me say I got a referral to a proctologist. Aha! Now the penny drops—try to keep up.

I'm not particularly fond of doctors, but occasionally, my wife realises I need to see one. It was with resigned truculence I paid a visit to the practice rooms of Dr Menuhin. He was the first proctologist I'd ever seen, and he enjoyed his work a little too much for my liking. I didn't much care for his name either—I suspected he may have been on the fiddle *(just when I thought the lame jokes had finished—Ed.)* However, the most disconcerting fact about him was that he had the hands of a navvy and fingers the size of Lebanese cucumbers.

Dr Menuhin wasn't content to have a good old rummage inside me with his cucumber fingers. Oh no, he wanted to get me into hospital and have a proper go at it. He told me it was a routine procedure that involved sending a camera up inside. It was at this point I had visions of a cameraman dressed in a wetsuit getting oiled up by his assistant. I didn't really want to go into hospital, but once I'd told my wife, I had little choice in the matter.

It was the most humiliating experience of my life! I'm not talking about the actual investigative procedure. I realise going up the rectum is a serious matter and nothing to joke about. What was humiliating was the preoperation routine. I assumed I would be given a private room with my own ensuite, considering certain things had to take place before the camera crew entered me. I consider myself pretty streetwise and clued up, but sometimes I can be a real thicko.

On arrival at the hospital, I sat in an overcrowded waiting room for thirty minutes. Eventually, a nurse appeared brandishing a clipboard. In a voice, which I'm confident was heard by all aboard the International Space Station, she yelled,

'Mr Northouse? Colonoscopy?' The crowded waiting room, which, until that point, had been a sombre tomb of boredom, now bristled with excitement. I hurriedly followed the nurse out of the room and into the hospital ward. Nope, no private room for me. She pointed to a bed on the end of a lengthy line of beds and said,

'Please get undressed and put the gown on and I'll be back in ten minutes.' I looked to my right and there was a row of reclining chairs occupied by people in various states of discombobulation. It was the post-operation recovery room. Some gawped at me with vacant expressions, wondering what time the film would begin. Others happily munched on egg sandwiches, and one or two looked like they needed urgent medical assistance. Directly opposite my bed was the door to the waiting room, a door that was wide open. A row of faces stared at me, waiting for a bit of free entertainment. I drew the curtains around my bed and disrobed. No sooner had I got my gown on and the nurse was back.

'Mr Northouse,' she barked at me, 'your gown is on back to front. The opening should be at the back.' Well, how was I to know, although considering the exploratory investigation I was about to undergo, it made sense.

'Ah! Okay,' I replied. 'If you could pop outside, I'll put it on the other way around.' The nurse huffed at this.

'Nonsense. You haven't got anything I haven't seen a million times before,' she responded impatiently. I felt like saying, "Okay, why don't you get your kit off, don't worry love, you've nothing I haven't seen before." However, the nurse was a woman of senior years, and I wasn't sure if that statement would hold water. Turning my back to her, I pulled the robe off and was about to put it on the correct way when I heard the swish of the curtains. The nurse was heading off down the corridor and had left the curtains open. Fascinated faces ogled my nakedness from the confines of the waiting room. I quickly pulled the curtains shut, put the robe on, and lay on the bed, contemplating the rich tapestry of life.

A few minutes passed before the nurse returned with a couple of plastic tubes.

'Okay, Mr Northouse, in a few minutes I'll be giving you an enema,' she boomed. 'It should be painless.' I'll be the judge of that, I thought. 'All you'll feel is a cold sensation in the bottom.'

Once again, she buggered off, leaving the curtains open. There was at least one redeeming part to this hospital farce, and it was the fact the nurse was elderly and female. I'm not sure I could have handled an attractive young nurse or God, forbid, a male nurse administering the enema. That may sound ageist or even sexist but I don't mean it like that. The nurse was more of a motherly or even grandmotherly figure, and her air of impatient indifference brought me some solace.

When the nurse returned, she asked me to roll onto my side and pull my knees up and into my chest. I heard the smack of rubber gloves being put on and an unfamiliar voice. I looked over my shoulder to notice another nurse in tow. A young nurse, an attractive young nurse. Strike me down. If it doesn't rain, it pours!

'Now, Mr Northouse, you don't mind if our junior nurse administers the enema, do you? They need to learn somewhere,' shouted the elderly nurse, as though she were working on the docks. Well, what choice did I have? My humiliation was now complete—or so I thought. The nurse was right, and she was wrong. Yes, it was cold, and no, it wasn't bloody painless. With the second tube inserted, rather roughly, in my opinion, I threw a quick glance over my shoulder. The damn curtain was slightly open again. There was now a crowd in the waiting room, all jostling for the best position. I swear I could hear a hawker drumming up business from the street outside.

'Roll up! Roll up! Step this way for the greatest show on earth!'

When the procedure was complete, the nurse informed me I had to keep the liquid in for as long as possible, at least fifteen minutes.

'Where's the toilet?' I asked. The nurse yanked the curtains fully open and pointed across the corridor to a door that backed into the waiting room.

The first couple of minutes were a breeze. By the third minute, there was a definite rumble in the jungle and by minute four, I was performing involuntary Kegels that would have got me a spot on the British Olympic Kegel Team.

I broke out in a cold sweat and realised I had only seconds before imminent disaster! I tentatively lifted myself off the bed and teetered out into the corridor. The problem was, my buttocks were so tightly clenched they could have split the atom. This prevented me from walking normally. The only way I could move was to keep my legs rigid with my feet splayed outwards. As I made my way across the corridor, I caught my reflection in the mirrored glass of the reception. I looked like a cross between an arthritic penguin and Frankenstein's monster.

Thankfully, I made it to the toilet and closed the door behind me. Worried murmurs from the waiting room hung in the air as two people stopped right outside the toilet door to engage in a nice little chat about the weather. There was no way I could hold on any longer.

I'll skip the details, but let's just say seismologists around the globe were frantically examining their seismographs to pinpoint the exact location of the tectonic shift which had occurred in the earth's plates. Tsunami warnings were duly issued for the Pacific Basin.

As I made my way back to the bed, I no longer cared my arse was on view for the world to see. I collapsed onto the bed with blessed relief. But not for long. As with earthquakes, there are often a few pre-tremors before the big one. Unbeknownst to me, the first visit to the lavatory was nothing but a pre-tremor.

The nurse returned and said I was doing well. Eight minutes had elapsed, only seven more to go. I informed her lift-off had already taken place some moments earlier. She looked disappointed in me, as though I'd let the team down. I aired my concerns about safely making a return trip to the toilet and suggested she put the Chemical Spill Team on red alert. I felt another unnatural sensation from down below and fully expected the Alien to erupt out of my midriff at any moment. And my nurse was no Sigourney Weaver. She smiled wearily at me as she handed me a giant nappy.

'Here, put this on,' she ordered. Under normal circumstances, I would have snorted derisively at her. Not on this occasion. The nappy went on in world record time.

I made my way back and forth to the toilet another four times. I walked as though rigor mortis had set in, and each time I passed the waiting room, I silently cursed the smirking faces.

Eventually, the storm abated. The nurse returned and gave me a pre-med and within minutes I was off with the pixies having a wonderful time. As they wheeled me into the operating theatre, I was happily whistling, "Doo Wah Diddy Diddy" by Manfred Man. The camera crew and production team were all waiting, dressed in wetsuits and greased up, but I didn't care anymore.

Keep Karma & Carry On

Book 2

Chapter 13

Ashes To Ashes

I t's birthday time! Yep, 12 months ago I published the first Discombobulated Newsletter. I looked back on the first edition the other day. It was exceedingly average. There was a small piece about why the newsletter is called "**Discombobulated**", a sentence about hessian underwear, and a link to a free book. Then it was goodnight Vienna and adios amigo.

I quickly realised if I wanted to engage with people, I had to make my newsletter interesting, entertaining, maybe even amusing, *(never mind, keep trying... you know what they say, if at first, you don't succeed—Ed).* Since then, it has morphed into something much bigger, like a mighty oak from an acorn (or an all-over body rash which started as a pimple... some might say). So, I better shut my big gob and get on with the job at hand and prove it. Without further ado, let's move on to this month's Mildly Interesting Fact.

Please ignore the idiot in parentheses, he's my editor, and he's a smartarse. I use the term "editor" in the widest possible sense, but he is cheap, well, free actually and until I can afford to pay a real editor, I have to put up with him *(I think you better start shopping around... Ed).*

Ashes to ashes, dust to dust... no, don't panic, I haven't gone all serious on you. This isn't about life and death, it's about something far more serious—Cricket. Wait, stop right there, don't hit the unsubscribe button, at least give it a go. I can guarantee you'll learn something *(What? from this newsletter? Ed)*

Imagine this; you are attending the Queen's garden party. You were invited because of your sterling efforts in protecting the environment, having managed to reduce the extinction rate of the lesser-spotted-moron. A singularly idiotic animal who likes to drive fast whilst texting on their phone, eating a bag of Cheezels and watching re-runs of the Antiques Roadshow on their in-car DVD player. An elderly gentleman, sporting a monocle, approaches from the rear, and introduces himself as Lord Smugly Brown Twinkletoes. He owns a small tract of land on the southwest coast of England called Cornwall. He says to you,

"I say, old chap, have you been watching the cricket, lately?" Well, thanks to this article, you will now be confident enough to engage the crusty old barmpot in conversation.

"Why, yes, it's been quite spiffing. I must say, I've been entranced by some magnificent googlies. And the chap with the third leg took an absolute jaffa of a catch yesterday." At which point, Lord Smugly, who is suitably impressed, and as mad as a pickled onion, may ask if you'd care to join him at his holiday home on the Tuscan Archipelago, which he also owns.

Very shortly, you will be lying on a sun-kissed beach with the Mediterranean lapping at your feet, whilst slurping on a Slippery Nipple (it's an alcoholic cocktail, for God's sake! Get your mind out of the gutter.) The only drawback to this paradise is that every forty-five minutes you have to rub coconut-infused suntan oil into Lord Smugly's buttocks— but hey, come on, you can't have a rainbow without any rain.

Now, where was I? Ah, yes, **The Ashes**. This is a cricketing contest between the fine, young, taut, well-honed cream of English cricket and a ragtag rabble of boozy miscreants from another country. I'm sorry, but when it comes to the Ashes, I'm extremely superstitious. I cannot actually mention the name of the opposing country or what the individuals who hail from that country are called. I'll refer to them as, **"Them"**.

For those of you who don't live in one of the Empire's colonial backwaters (sorry, I meant Commonwealth Countries) I will give you some clues as to this colony, I meant country. They have Blokes and Sheila's. They like a drink (or twelve) as they throw prawns onto the barbie. They change their Prime Minister more often than the Brits (that's going some...), eat one of their national emblems when it's not tied down, Bruce, and say the phrase, *"Fair dinkum cobber, strewth, true blue, ridgy-didge, dinky dye, yeah, yeah, nah mate,"* often. That's right, I'm talking about New Zealanders... no, I'm not, I'm joking. The Kiwis are a completely different block of fruit and nut altogether. *(Hang on... what was the loud bang I heard? Oh, don't worry, it was only the unsubscribe button exploding—Ed).*

Why is it called the Ashes? I can hear my American friends and Zorg from Norway ask? Because England lost the very first match between the two countries. To be beaten, by **"Them"**, was considered the death of English cricket. In response to this catastrophic event, the English burnt the umpires and put their ashes into an old perfume jar—well, they were tiny umpires. *That is how the Ashes were born.*

Every four years, they come over here, and every four years we go over to **"Them"**. Obviously, not at the same time otherwise, you'd have eleven cricketers stood around scratching their heads at opposite sides of the world, saying, "They did say Thursday, at eleven, didn't they?"

To me, cricket is the ultimate sporting event. The Ashes, the pinnacle of the sport. Let's look at some reasons why. For a sport, it is very sophisticated. It is played over five days—nice!

It starts at 11 am and play continues for two hours. The game then stops for forty minutes while everyone has lunch. The English nibble on cucumber sandwiches and sip iced tea from porcelain cups sprinkled with gold leaf. They discuss the weather, flower arranging and the fall in the share price of Werther's Originals.

The other mob, "**Them**", get stuck into half a pig's arse wedged between two bread vans, washed down with a bucket of Fosters Thunderbox beer. They don't discuss anything but merely grunt as they stick their batting coach's head down the toilet and repeatedly flush it. Apparently, it's great fun—although I think the batting coach may disagree.

Play resumes for another two hours before it stops for afternoon tea. The above rituals are repeated. There's a final two hours of play, into the early evening, then everyone goes home for the day and plays charades, apart from "**Them**" who prefer to go "cow tipping".

This continues for five days, after which, more often than not, the game is a draw. This process is repeated five times over the forthcoming months. You see? It's sporting perfection incarnate.

My wife hates cricket, especially the Ashes. She knows it is one of my joys in life, and during the Ashes, I am given leave of absence to do bugger all. There may be a dangerous tree branch swaying over my daughter's bedroom,

"Simon, dearest, do you think you could remove that life-threatening branch before it kills someone?"

"The Ashes are on. I'll take care of it in seven weeks."

"Do you think it's possible to reattach the front door to its hinges, it can get awfully draughty on a night?"

"No problem, I'll do it at the end of September."

Having read this, you may think the Ashes is a game between a bunch of simpering sops and a band of bellicose braggarts. It's not. Cricketers are supreme athletes with massive reserves of endurance. They are highly skilled and have nerves of steel.

Cricket is human chess. There are bluffs, counter bluffs, foiling tactics, skill, patience, aggression, sandpaper, attack, and counterattack. It's like an ancient battle fought on green fields and dusty tracks.

I realise some of you will have found more interesting things to do, like repainting your underwear, than read about cricket—but more fool you. It won't be you on the Tuscan Island, half-cut and smelling of coconut oil.

Your loss, not mine.

Chapter 14

Sex Robots

D id you know that as early as 2025 it will be common for middle-income families to have a sex robot in their home? I bet that made you choke on your cornflakes. *(What the hell have you been researching this last month? Ed).*

What would make me come out with such a statement? Well, recently, I was channel surfing and came across a documentary about sex robots. It was as interesting as it was disturbing. Yes, sex robots are on the rise (pardon the pun, madam). Apart from their obvious use (and abuse), they can offer companionship, advice, learn to laugh at your jokes and it is believed by 2050, it will be legal to marry your robot, although why anyone would want to ruin a perfectly good relationship baffles me.

For transparency's sake, let me state I am not in the market for a sex robot... unless anyone has a second-hand one going cheap—calm down, I'm joking. I have no need for a sex robot. I am very satisfied with my sex life, although I am developing RSI in the wrists and my forearms are starting to resemble Popeye's. However, I digress. Where was I?

Ah yes, robots of the sexual variety. All this got me thinking. If it becomes the norm and acceptable to have a sex robot in the home, would I actually want one? *I'm a man—of course I would!* But I thought a bit deeper, and on second thoughts, no, I wouldn't want one, and for many good reasons.

I could never bring myself to have sex with a robot, although thinking back to some of my former girlfriends, I can easily imagine what it would be like, robotic. My worry with artificial intelligence is it could potentially self-learn. The first six months would be fine, and Miss Robot (let's call her Demi) accepts all my advances. But I can see the day when I make my move on Demi only to be rebuffed with, "not tonight dear, my batteries are low," or "for God's sake, we only did it two months ago! Can't you sort yourself out?"

It's bad enough being refused entry from a real person, but imagine the humiliation of being knocked back by titanium, latex and a lithium battery. My fragile male ego would be shattered.

I'd also worry about it malfunctioning. What if halfway through the deed, Demi suddenly closed up shop? You'd have a hell of a job explaining that when you front up to accident and emergency with a Demi Moore lookalike robot attached like a limpet to your spam javelin. The old, "Yes, Doctor, that's correct, I slipped as I was getting out of the shower," is not going to wash with anyone this time.

What if it got to the point where the robot was so intelligent, it could manufacture its own womb? I come home from a hard day's night at the pickling factory, only to be greeted with, "You're going to be a daddy!" Knowing my luck, it would probably be septuplets and I'd be running around like a headless chicken cleaning up after seven R2 bleeding D2s. And don't even think about sex now—that's gone right out of the window. I'd have to up-size the house, the car, my wallet. There'd be no more candlelit dinners for me and Demi. We'd be too busy cleaning up puke, extricating small objects from mouths, and changing batteries. The whole thing is a nightmare!

What would I buy them for Christmas and birthdays? I couldn't give them a robot. That would be weird. I'd have to buy them a small human to play with, even more expense. What would I say to them when I took them to the beach and all the other kids are swimming in the sea? "Daddy, why aren't we allowed in the sea?"

"Because you'll spontaneously self-combust, Alpha 5. Now run along and build a replica Guggenheim Bilbao sandcastle with Andromeda and Hal. And stop calling all the other kids thickos. It's not nice, even though it is true."

One morning, when I get home from my night shift as a pork scratching tester (that's right, I have to work two jobs now), I notice a letter on the table. It turns out while I've been working my butt off, Demi has been enjoying a ménage à trois with the cordless vacuum cleaner and microwave oven. It transpires they've all run off together to live on Fantasy Island, "Da plane, da plane" indeed. I've now lost the love of my life; the carpets are filthy, and I have nothing to defrost my Cumberland sausage on a morning. Could it get any worse? Well, yes, it bloody well could!

It turns out all my offspring are female, and I'll have seven weddings to fork out for. Not only that, but because they're wi-fied to Google, it means I'll never win another game of Scrabble. No, I'm afraid a sex robot is not for me. I'd much prefer a chore robot who can do all those tedious little jobs for me, like cutting the grass, fetching me a beer, and answering the phone from telesales people. That's what the world needs.

Chapter 15

The Complaint Email

My wife is a brilliant complainer. I don't mean it in a nasty way. She isn't forever complaining, well, only to me. What I mean is when she complains she's so damn jolly and nice about it. By the time she's finished on the phone talking to the telephone company about being overcharged, she now has a new best pal in the customer service girl who took her call. They've already agreed to meet up for coffee, go on a shopping spree together and they've friended each other on Facebook within seconds. She always, always, extracts an apology and gets a reimbursement. It's bloody annoying, actually.

Me? Well, that's a different kettle of asparagus. First up, being British, I rarely complain. I grit my teeth and quietly seethe thinking of all the things I'd like to do to the clown who put anchovies on my Hawaiian pizza. My wife says things like,

"Tell the waiter. I'm sure they'll change it if you ask." At which point I break out into a cold sweat and clench my buttocks so tightly I'm in danger of exploding.

"No! It's fine. I'll eat it. Anchovies are full of Omega 3. It will be good for me."

"But you won't enjoy it," she'll say, as she stuffs another slice of anchovy free pizza into her mouth.

"That's not the point," I declare defiantly, not actually sure what the point is.

I never complain in person, and I've even stopped complaining by phone as I tend to get carried away. The last time I did, I fully expected a SWAT team to descend from a helicopter and launch stun grenades through my windows. No, I only complain by email now. It's a far more dignified way to conduct oneself.

I compose my first draft, then let it simmer for a couple of hours. When I return, I carefully remove all the expletives and threats, which usually leaves me with,

"Dear Sir or Madam," and "Yours sincerely—Simon Northouse." After draft five, it's ready to go.

A couple of years ago, we had our annual family holiday in the UK. Yes, I know, I can hear thousands of you screaming, "WHY?" It would have worked out cheaper to have a glamping holiday on top of Mount Kilimanjaro and be spoon-fed caviar by the Queen's butler.

However, I digress. Actually, there were only two things which slightly marred the holiday. The first happened while I was sitting outside a fantastic pub in a place called Beaumaris on the Isle of Anglesey in North Wales (if you haven't visited, put it on your bucket list). A seagull shat in my pint of Guinness. This sort of thing can scar a man for life. Having to pour a pint of Guinness down the drain was one of the hardest things I've ever had to do. From that moment on, I realised I had the fortitude and resolve to achieve anything.

The second incident happened when I had to return the hire car to Leeds and Bradford Airport. I'd almost forgotten about this nightmarish event until the other day. I was cleaning out my inbox on Gmail and came across a folder called "Complaints". Inside was an email I had sent to the hire car company after they had bombarded me with "Customer Satisfaction Survey" forms for weeks. I have reproduced the missive here to show you the correct way to complain via email.

"Dear LameCar,

After persistently assaulting my inbox with your "Customer Satisfaction" survey, I have taken the time to reply to you. Before I begin, I would like to point out the erroneous title of your survey. You should really have two forms, the "Customer Satisfaction" form and the "Customer Fucking Pissed Off" form. If you had, I would be filling out the latter now.

Okay, where do I begin? I suppose at the beginning. The vehicle pick-up from Heathrow Airport was relatively pain-free, apart from being repeatedly asked if I wished to pay extra to annul the insurance excess. At one point, I suspected your Customer Service Rep was actually a robot whose voice chip had malfunctioned.

Now to the car. The shoebox on wheels (the Micro Fiat) was also fine, albeit a little cramped for a family of four. This is my fault for being a cheapskate. However, if I had realised the car was designed by children under the age of six, for children under the age of six, I may have upgraded to something slightly larger, such as a unicycle. I now know how those clowns feel who ride around under the big top in their Noddy cars. However, it was only required for twenty-four hours to get us from A to B before we swapped it for a "grown-ups" vehicle.

Now to the unpleasant part. I arranged to return the car to your depot at Leeds and Bradford Airport within twenty-four hours. This experience was probably the worst of my life—and rest assured, I've plenty to choose from.

Firstly, the signage for returning hire cars is virtually non-existent at Leeds and Bradford Airport. I missed the postage-stamp-sized sign on the way in and ended up in the short-stay car park.

If you are unaware, this is the type of car park which you can happily drive in to, unhindered and park up. However, to get out of the car park, one has to pay. The thirty seconds I was in there cost me £6, as it did my wife, who was following behind in the "grown-ups" car. Already, I'm £12 down.

From my expensive vantage point in the short-stay car park, I could see various hire car signs in the distance, their flags waving enticingly in the bitterly cold wind and rain. However, trying to navigate to them was like searching for the entrance to Eldorado. I eventually made it to the long-stay car park and parked up. I then began some reconnaissance. I walked on foot to the hire car drop off point (in the pouring rain) to figure out how to drive there. In the meantime, my wife, much akin to a homing pigeon, had managed to return to the short-stay car park. This cost her another £6 to get out of. I'm now £18 down in the space of five minutes.

After my reconnaissance mission, I jotted down extensive notes and drew a map to help me achieve my objective of navigating to the drop-off point. Eventually, with the help of NASA, I managed to drive the car into the covert entrance of the hire car return depot.

I would have thought, for my commendable efforts, there may have been a red carpet rolled out for me and a marching band playing "It's a long way to Tipperary". But alas, this was not the case. In fact, the place appeared deserted.

I parked up and spent ten minutes (in the pouring rain) wandering around like a comatose vagrant looking for the LameCar representative. When I eventually stumbled across his or her little kiosk, to my dismay, I found it locked up.

After a few more minutes of staggering around in the increasing wind and freezing rain, I spotted a Hertz car representative. He informed me LameCar doesn't employ a "returns" rep on the weekends. Of course they don't—why would they? I mean, what person in their right mind would ever need to drop a car off on a Saturday? The very thought is preposterous!

The Hertz man (who does work weekends, oddly enough) told me I would have to make my way to the main terminal where LameCar had a kiosk inside. It was with a certain amount of resigned fatalism that I glanced at the terminal in the distance—the very far distance. I was hoping my wife could drive me there, as I was experiencing the first signs of hypothermia. However, I noticed she'd already exited the short-stay car park and immediately turned onto the one-way loop that leads directly back to the short-stay car park, for reasons that to this day, have never been fully explained.

She was now caught in a cross between Ground Hog Day and some Kafkaesque nightmare. Despite the roar of jet engines overhead, I could still clearly make out her expletives drifting in the wind, some of which I'd never heard before. I doubt the architect who designed the short-stay car park ever envisaged the day when someone would visit it three times in ten minutes. Ka-ching! That, by the way, was the sound of another £6 debited from my credit card.

I walked the 1 km to the main terminal (in the pouring rain, and now blizzard conditions) in a mood that could best be described as "apoplectic". Once inside the terminal, I made my way to the LameCar kiosk.

I apologise for bothering your rep on that morning. He was busy on the phone talking to what sounded like his "Bookie". I never did check to see whether "Fool's Errand" won the 3:30 at Aintree. Your rep briefly broke off to tell me, "Leave the keys there, buddy." This was probably a blessing in disguise as if dialogue had broken out between us, I may now be holidaying at one of Her Majesties retirement villages.

There were no forms to sign, no check of the vehicle for damage, no thank you or even a "kiss my blue arse". This whole dreadful experience took over forty-five minutes, exactly how one likes to spend their time when on *holiday*.

My wife was now waiting for me in the long-stay car park. Soaked to the skin, suffering from frostbite and hypothermia, I entered the warm comfort of the car with a certain amount of relief. As we left the long-stay car park, my wife once again turned onto the one-way loop that leads to the short-stay car park. I'm not sure this was a mistake. I think she had grown quite fond of the short-stay car park and wanted to bid it farewell one last time. Another £6.

The nightmare was not yet over. I had made the fatal schoolboy error of forgetting to fill the fuel tank up with petrol before returning the Noddy car. You took the liberty of rectifying this error by filling it up yourselves and debiting my credit card. I'm not exactly sure which petrol station you used to replenish the car. Possibly it was in a parallel universe where the cost of fuel is 36% more expensive than it is in our universe. Apparently, it took 23 litres to fill the car up. (I'm not sure the shoebox on wheels could even hold 23 litres—and it was half full when I dropped it off.) The average price of petrol I had bought during my journey from London to Leeds was £1.80. Apparently, your mystery service station, on planet Zorg, charges £2.30 a litre. I suggest you shop around in future.

Your mark-up of 50 pence per litre, multiplied by 23 litres, cost me £11.50. Oh, and just to put one last cherry on top of the cake, you charged me VAT at 20% on top of it, a cost of £2.30.

As petrol already has VAT built into the price, I think your little scam may be illegal. You cannot charge a tax on something which has already been taxed. This is a matter I will raise with the Inland Revenue Tax Office, although I foresee my dealings with them will be about as enjoyable and fruitful as my dealings with you.

With the cost of petrol, the illegal tax and the car park fees, I was out of pocket to the tune of £82.900—which is more than double what the damn Noddy car cost me to hire in the first place!

You may call this vertical integration or some other such "management" wank-word, but I call it price gouging the customer.

I will not be using your company again and I would appreciate reimbursement of £82.90. There is no charge for the laundromat used to dry my clothes or for the 45 minutes of my time, my wife's time or my long-suffering children's time. I'm sure when I told them we were going to the UK for our holiday, they never envisaged the delights of the short-stay car park at Leeds and Bradford Airport. Who needs Disneyland?

I look forward to never using you again.

Yours insincerely,

Mr Northouse

P.S. I left my Sound of Music CD in the Noddy car CD player. Is there any chance you could forward this on to me? I do so miss the Von Trapp's unbridled joy and enthusiasm for life despite the fact their country has recently been annexed and the hills are now alive to the roar of Panzer Tanks and the click of jackboots. It just goes to show—in times of adversity, it pays to keep one's chin up.

Needless to say, I never received a reply, nor did I get my Sound of Music CD back. It irks me somewhat to think an employee of LameCar is right now, happily singing "raindrops on roses and whiskers on kittens", at my expense.

Chapter 16

Fathers

H ere's a quote for you.

"I believe that what we become depends on what our fathers teach us at odd moments when they aren't trying to teach us. We are formed by little scraps of wisdom." - Umberto Eco.

Until recently, I thought Umberto Eco was the new Toyota electric car, but apparently not. Mr Eco was a novelist, professor, literary critic, and philosopher. I stumbled across his quote while searching the internet for a new drive belt for my washing machine. I find it slightly odd he only references fathers and not mothers (or even grandparents). I'm pretty damn sure there are millions of adults out there who were raised solely by their mothers or by their grandparents. Maybe he was reflecting on his own experience.

I'm not yet regarded as a great philosopher *(give it time sunshine, give it time—Ed)* but I would bet my left testicle that as many mothers have had a similar effect upon their offspring (for better or worse) as fathers (for better or worse.) This brings me neatly onto this month's mildly interesting fact.

Did you know that fathers who share household chores with their wives tend to have more ambitious daughters? The word "tend" does somewhat undermine the claim this is a fact, but it's on Google so it must be true.

Here's another fact, "father seahorses are the only male animals to become pregnant." There's so much wrong with this statement I don't know where to begin. It doesn't explain how daddy seahorse became pregnant. Was it mummy seahorse who got father seahorse up the duff?

Did she stagger in from the pub late one night and suggest a quickie on the kitchen table, ignoring his protestations that he'd missed his pill? I'm also certain not all male seahorses become pregnant. What about those unfortunate ones who look more like seadonkeys than seahorses? Ms Lady Seahorse isn't going to strut her stuff with him, not unless she's desperate or he's extremely wealthy.

Anyway, I seem to have gone off track slightly. Ah, that's right, fathers and daughters. I was having an unusual conversation with my teenage daughter the other day. When I say "unusual" I don't mean the subject was unusual—no, I meant it was unusual we were having an "actual" conversation, as in two people speaking to each other. Okay, I'm exaggerating somewhat. It was more of a monologue, i.e. me speaking. I said something amusing to her *(what a novel idea! You should try it in your books sometime—Ed.)* She found my little take on life quite funny. Without any hint of sarcasm or irony, she replied,

"LOL". It was obviously too much effort for her to physically laugh or even smile. Far simpler to say, "LOL". My reaction was predictable.

"WTF!" I initialised, adding the exclamation mark with a downward stroke of my index finger.

She looked a little discombobulated for a nanosecond before responding with, "Sup bro?"

I shrugged, held a palm out in exasperation, shook my head and said, "OMG! Like, duh!"

"Evs" were her parting words as she navigated through the dining room, bypassing the dog, the cat and the man stood on a ladder polishing the crystal chandeliers, while her eyes were super-glued to her phone.

I call this phone-weave. The ability to move safely in your environment whilst your brain and senses are disengaged. It's like a new sixth sense for anyone under thirty. Okay, I understand some of you will be shaking your heads thinking,

"Has he overdosed on Viagra and St John's Wort again? I've read the paragraph back five times, and it still doesn't make sense." For those who haven't fully grasped the newish language of Textlish, I'll translate.

Dad says something mildly amusing. Daughter says LOL (laugh out loud). I say, "What the fu@k!" She looks confused by my reaction and asks, "Pray, father dear, whatever seems to be the matter with you?" (i.e. sup bro or what is up brother?). I shake my head in consternation, but she is already bored with proceedings as something new has appeared on "TikTok" (don't ask!).

She departs with "Evs" meaning "whatever". You see, even "whatever", which used to be the shortened form of "DILIGAF" (do I look like I give a fu@k) has now been shortened to "evs".

I believe my daughter is waiting for the day when they invent the hologram microchip. That way, she won't ever have to speak again. She can communicate via her hologram emojis.

"Have you emptied the dishwasher yet? I know it's only five hours ago since I first asked you, but..." Her tired smiley face will flash annoyance or maybe even anger.

She's now got a boyfriend and seems to have taken up residency at his family's abode. I assume she doesn't get asked to empty the dishwasher while over there. Her boyfriend seems to be a nice enough lad, but I find it odd that at the age of seventeen he still plays on a scooter. I'm not talking about a Vespa or a Lambretta, but a scooter you push along with one foot.

When I was seventeen, I was on a building site surrounded by hairy-arsed bricklayers. They'd send me to the store for a long weight, a left-handed hammer and don't forget the skyline and box of skyhooks. Yep, I actually fell for it. Oh, the adroit wit of the working-class man. After work, I would head out to the pub with my mates where we'd chat, play pool, and occasionally get into scrapes. Some nights we'd head to a nightclub and boogie the night away. **Intermission:** My wife has just read this and reliably informed me the last person to use the word "boogie" died in 1987. I do apologise.

When my father was seventeen, he was servicing engines on Spitfires and Hurricanes—while they were in the air, or so he says. When my grandfather was seventeen, he was holidaying in France at a quaint little place near the River Somme. In between quaffing strawberry daiquiris and gorging on Camembert, he was loading shells into a howitzer and dodging bullets that had "Made in Germany" stamped on them.

I know, it's me, I'm getting old. I'm slowly turning into my father. It won't be long before I'm complaining about modern music and long hair while adjusting my flat cap in the mirror. It's not that I don't know what's going on. I understand all the modern ways and all the latest apps and gizmos. Facebook, Instagram, Pinterest, WhatsApp, TikTok, PayPal, Netscape Navigator, texting, sexting, dogging, toothing. I've even used an Uber. I know how they work and what they are used for. I use some of them myself to publicise my books. But the truth is, I hate them all with a passion. They are time vampires, sucking the minutes from my life whilst offering little in return—well, apart from the dogging apps.

I believe children these days grow up too quickly and stay adolescent too long. Here's how it used to work:

0–12 = Child; 13–16 = Adolescent; 16–21 = Young man / woman; 21–50 = Man / woman; 50+ = Grumpy old bastard.

It was the natural order of things and seemed to work well. Today, children become adolescents at about the age of eight and stay that way for another twenty years. They completely bypass the young man/woman stage and have a few years of maturity before hitting the Grumpy Old Bastard phase by age thirty-three.

But I digress. Back to Umberto Eco. So, according to him, we become what our fathers unwittingly taught us. I've thought about this for a while and realised there's some truth to it. I have learned the following from my father: never fall asleep while the chip pan is on or while sunbathing. Never buy my wife an ironing board for her birthday or a new vacuum cleaner for Christmas. Never assume in a road-rage incident with a small car, the driver of the small car is also going to be small. Always turn the electricity off before changing a light bulb during a thunderstorm. And lastly, never pick a fight with a cat—there's only one winner there—malevolent psychopaths that they are. Thank you, Umberto.

Chapter 17

Meppy Eastmas

I f you're anything like me, you're probably over Christmas by about
November 15th. The sales pitch is relentless, and the barrage begins
earlier and earlier. At some point, Easter and Christmas are going to clash.
Yesterday, in the supermarket, I noticed they already had hot-cross buns on
sale. Another week and the Easter eggs will be on display.

Why at Xmas do we eat things we never eat during the other 11 months
and 19 days of the year? When was the last time you came home after a hard
day's night pickling herrings and thought to yourself,

"Hmm, I could murder a few walnuts, some dates and a warm glass of
mulled wine." Probably never?

There are a few things I am partial to at Christmas. Terry's Chocolate
Oranges, After Eight Mints and the hope that Kylie Minogue pops up
somewhere dressed in an elf costume. But once again, I only ever eat these
delicacies at Yuletide, (obviously not Kylie Minogue in an elf costume.
That could get me into all sorts of bother. Okay, let's move on, there's
nothing to see here).

Normally, when I drop into my friend's house, he'll offer me a cold
refreshing beer. But even he seems to take leave of his senses during
Festivus. I called around last night, and he asked me if I'd care for a wee
glass of sherry or port. I politely thanked him for his offer then told him to
stop being a bell-end and fetch me a cleansing ale... oh, and a plate of
Brussel sprouts to go with it.

Well, Christmas is nearly over then we can all get back to normality (whatever that is). Only one more hurdle to stumble over... New Year's Eve. I've never really understood why, once a year, normal, rational people suddenly become drunken, emotional morons for a few hours. Do they really believe the ticking of a clock from 11:59:59 to 12:00:00 unshackles the chains of misery, confusion, debt, worry and bad habits of the previous year? They act like they've won the Lotto jackpot and that when they awake in the morning, they'll be served croissants in bed by Nicole Kidman in a Catwoman outfit (or Hugh Jackman or both, if that's your bag).

The reality is, they'll stumble out of bed with a cracking hangover and wince when they recall how they kissed the woman with the hairy goitre tenderly on the neck and told her beauty is only skin deep.

I'm not a curmudgeon *(can we have a vote on that? Ed.)* But I can't wait for the mind-numbing drudgery of everyday life to return. I understand for some people this is a spiritual time of reflection. For others, it's about spending time with their loved ones or even family. Me? I'm far shallower than that. It's about watching the Boxing Day Test match (cricket) for seven hours followed by the original version of "The Italian Job" while nibbling on a wafer-thin mint. Remember, in the immortal words of Michael Caine, "You were only supposed to blow the bloody doors off!" Wise words indeed.

Chapter 18

Big Buttocks

It's been a while since we had any Latin, so mull this one over, "Clunibus Magnis". A rough translation means big buttocks, or buttocks big if you're that way inclined. It is an interesting fact that about ten years ago the most frequent search term typed into Google was, "How to reduce the size of my bum?" Today the most frequent search term is "How to increase the size of my bum?"

Apparently, it's all Kim Kardashian's fault. Going back several years, I didn't even know who Kim K was. To tell you the truth, I'm not much the wiser now. However, my daughters were all over it. They'd be sitting transfixed to the goggle box, watching Kim and her associates as they did incredibly interesting things. Here's Kim getting out of bed. Now she's eating her breakfast while glued to her phone. Now she's getting her nails done. And oh my God... she's put something in the microwave oven. I can see why the show was such a hit. When I posed the question, "Who is Kim Kardashian?" My daughters both laughed hysterically at me.

"Dad, you're so lame. Everyone knows who Kim Kardashian is? She's the most famous woman in the world!" I had a "Hmm..." moment. A few other women did spring to mind I'd consider more famous. The Queen, Princess Di, Mother Teresa, Mavis Crotchgape from the pork dripping shop. Mavis was quite well known around my parts... I mean, around my area. Hang on... I'll start again. Mavis was very well known around town and had quite a reputation. The way she handled a Cumberland sausage was poetry in motion. Anyway, I digress.

When I inquired why KK was famous, my daughters informed me she was famous for being famous. Not only that, but she was married to the other world-famous celeb I'd never heard of, "Yanke Stew". Sorry, I had a sudden bout of dyslexia—I meant, "Kanye West". Anyway, apparently, KK has or had a large bottom. I don't mean large, as in it trailed on the floor behind her, I mean large, as in tight, firm, plump. The sort of bottom that if you flicked it with your finger, it would let out a high pitched "ping" and you'd end up with a fractured digit.

When I was younger and I was going out for the night with my wife, she would always pose the question,

"Does my bum look big in this?" as she craned her head over her shoulder, staring suspiciously in the mirror. Now, I'm a quick learner. I learnt early on that if there was a pause before me answering "No" not only would I get the silent treatment for about a month but worse, I'd also lose a good hour's valuable drinking time as she tried on another thirty dresses. So by the time the last syllable of her word "this" had left her lips, I would offer an emphatic "No!"

Today it's different. When she asks, "Does my bum look big in this?" I reply, "Yes" to which she says, "Good!" Who said husbands can't evolve? The rules of combat change all the time and one must keep abreast of the latest developments to ensure a happy home. I use the word "happy" in the broadest possible sense.

What was I talking about? *(good question... I'm afraid I can't help you out. I nodded off momentarily—Ed)*. Ah, yes... big bums and famous for being famous, Kimmy.

I hope she doesn't mind me calling her Kimmy. She does read this newsletter, and she's one of my biggest fans... that's if it's the same KK.

Actually Kimmy did something in 2014 which did warrant her being famous. She broke the internet. I assumed she must have sat on it by accident. But no, the truth (broadest possible sense—again) was quite different. She posed for the cover of "Paper" magazine.

As part of the intensive and meticulous research I undertake to bring you these facts, I have been studying the photo in great detail. In fact, I studied it for so long I became temporarily "bog-eyed" for a couple of days which not only gave me a passing resemblance to Marty Feldman but also scared the hell out of the dog. *(No one under the age of 99 will know who Marty Feldman was—Ed).*

There's another thing I've noticed about Kim, apart from her gravity-defying derriere. Her head is on backwards. In every photo I've seen of Kim, her back is to the camera, yet her head is facing the camera. It's either an unfortunate congenital defect or she grew up in a circus. I suppose it comes in handy when she's parallel parking.

So big, firm bottoms are all the rage thanks to Kimmy. If you've got nothing better to do with your life, try this: type into Google, "Kim K Ass". Google tells me there are over 98 million results. That's a lot of arse pics to get through but I have a spare hour after I've finished this newsletter to make a start. By the way, you may want to Google search in a "private window" or "incognito" mode. What you consider legitimate research could be misconstrued as "pervy" by others. Some people always assume the worst.

Chapter 19

They're Only Words

I love words, most of the time. However, certain words and phrases become flavour of the month or even the decade. They are overused, misrepresentative of what they originally meant, and become bloody annoying every time you hear them. I've taken it upon myself to point these words out. If there was an "X-Factor" (overused) for words, then these are the guys and gals who look good, sound good, but ultimately are rather like a Pavlova—you know, all trousers no zip, all shop-front no door —if you get my drift *(which we don't—Ed)*.

Most of these words or phrases are used by the media or the commentariat. If they are not nipped in the bud at birth, *(mixed metaphors —Ed)* then everyone starts using them—God forbid!

Okay, first up: **Unprecedented**: I can guarantee if you watch the national news tonight on TV, the word, "unprecedented" will be said at least three times. Everything these days is "unprecedented". The word actually means "without precedent" i.e. it's never happened before. According to those reading the news, we can have "unprecedented" violence, weather, sporting comebacks, giant strawberries, and repercussions. Unprecedented is the "new" absolutely. I hate it with a passion.

The next one is a phrase: **A Once In A Hundred Year Event**: You can interchange the word "event" with, storm, flood, wind, fire or any other climatic condition you can think of. It's amazing how many times I've watched the news, only to be told, "It was a once in a hundred-year flood," only to be informed a week later that the same place received another "...

once in a hundred-year flood." You can't have two different events, hitting the same place, with the same climatic conditions and call it a "once in a hundred-year event". It only happened a fortnight ago!

Only the other day, my wife used the word unprecedented, which was quite unprecedented. I'd collected a few things together that needed washing, threw them in the washing machine and hit the hot cycle. A couple of hours later, I heard a hell of a ruckus emanating from the laundry, so went to investigate. My wife held up a red dog blanket in one hand, in the other, a slew of bras and knickers.

"You dickhead!" she yelled (amongst other things which I cannot repeat here).

"Is there a problem?" I politely enquired.

"Yes! I only bought these bras and knickers today!"

"Your point being?"

"My point being, they were white!"

"You don't like pink?"

Then she said it. "This is unprecedented, even by your standards!"

"Aha," I replied, "it's not unprecedented. Have you forgotten about your white blouse and the black towels? Anyway, don't worry, it's a once in a hundred-year event." I'm still suffering from tinnitus.

Chapter 20

Retired Husband Syndrome

A s some of you will be aware, I like to do intensive and extensive research when developing my books, my plots, my characters (*go on... Pinocchio—Ed*). Only yesterday, I was searching the internet looking for information on mental disorders (*therapy? Ed*). Ignore him, I do.

I have a character in a forthcoming book who may, or may not, suffer from the "fear of loss". I was trying to find out if there was a medical term for this, you know, like a Latin definition—Fearius Lossius or Fuciius Nota Againius.

During my research, I came across something which made me laugh. Now, laughing at mental illness is no laughing matter. I take the subject seriously. However, this particular fear, phobia, affliction knocked me off my chair for a few seconds.

Apparently, this disorder is prevalent in Japanese women of a certain age. I'm not sure if I have any followers in Japan (*if you do, you won't after this —Ed*) but many Japanese women develop an affliction termed "Retired Husband Syndrome" or, RHS for short.

You see, Japanese men spend a lot of time at work, a ridiculously long amount of time at work, compared to say, the western world, where we try to spend as little time at work as possible. Even when we are at work, we will do anything to avoid "actual" work.

I've made idle chit-chat with people I dislike. The sort of people who, if you were given a choice of five minutes in their company or a visit to the clap clinic, you'd be jumping in a taxi and heading to STD Inc every time.

I've visited the toilet to study the latest football results, become quite competent at cryptic crosswords (those damn things can take hours to finish) and I've even snuck out of the fire exit for a game of golf and had a game of online scrabble with Dave from accounts—who struggled to write his first name; you name it—I've done it, to avoid work.

Anyway, back to retired husband syndrome. So, these Japanese ladies can spend 30-40 years home alone. Husband leaves at 5 am. Finishes work at 8 pm. Visits a Geisha bar and gets drunk on sake. Returns home at 10 pm, eats his dinner, goes to bed.

The day finally arrives when he retires. The husband is now home all day. After 40 years, the wife has evolved a system, a damn good system. In fact, everything runs like clockwork. What time of day to go shopping, how to save money, pay the bills on time, repaint the house, develop an extensive vegetable garden, rear hens for free eggs, play bingo every Tuesday evening, play hide the sausage with the muscular gardener every Wednesday and Friday afternoon. She has it all sorted, no problemo! Life is sweet—until... Mr Yokoshimo Miserygutso collects his pension.

Now it all turns to shit! Why? Because Mr Miserygutso was the middle-manager for a company that manufactures the bristles in toothbrushes. And a very successful company it was too. Plus, Mr Miserygutso was very good at his job, or so he says to anyone that will listen.

He organised many meetings (thousands) to talk about himself, what he did, how important he was, and how without him, the world would have ended twenty-seven years ago. He was the perfect, archetypal middle-manager.

Now he's retired, he decides (after 40 years) his home is not run as efficiently as it could be and therefore it requires an Internal Management Review.

He conducts an audit, a time and motion study, a fiscal review and an end-of-year employee performance evaluation (on his wife).

After eight months, and many hands-on meetings with himself, he finally produces his 800-page white and blue-paper review.

"Moving Forward, Together: Into the Millennium—The Journey Continues in Unprecedented Times". The summary of his 800-page document states:

"At present, this abode does not meet stakeholder expectations or senior management (me) core competencies. As such, I intend to implement a radical agenda to reduce waste, improve efficiency, and drive forward, compatible, multi-integrated policies which will immunise the abode from continuing market fluctuations and volatility, long into the future, so providing value equity within difficult pyjamas.

With immediate effect, we will discontinue the policy of purchasing Cosmopolitan, expensive toilet paper and those wooden paddles to stir your coffee with. This will free up finances for extra bean sprouts, pickled gherkins, and sake. There may also be opportunities for existing employees to evaluate their long-term direction and take the next step into achieving positive outcomes by positioning themselves into a wider, worldwide market, which is now truly global.

A five-year plan is forthcoming. Unfortunately, this has been delayed because my integrated computerised portal (i.e. laptop) has become infected with Lady-Boy porn and pasta carbonara recipes.

I have taken due diligence to expedite this matter. A meeting with the "IT Security Department" (Mr Feeverwanki from the sushi shop next door) has been arranged for tomorrow morning. I will also be seeking advice from Mistress Fugly, from the local English pie and mash shop, to discuss my carbonara infection.

Yours sincerely,

Mr Miserygutso—Team Leader and former head of the Bristles Department of Toothbrushes 'R' Us (Japanese affiliate).

The veggie garden is replaced with a putting green. The washing line is removed from outside the laundry door and a tumble-dryer is installed in the hen house. The hens are pissed off with this and decide to move out. Luckily, someone on Airbnb, called "Sly", offers them a free perch for the night at "Foxhotel Coop - stay one night free and you'll never leave."

By now the wife has developed Retired Husband Syndrome. The symptoms include gnashing of teeth, frustration, annoyance, anger, hatred, and cutting the left leg off all Mr Miserygutso's trousers.

Meanwhile, after implementing his radical new agenda, Mr Miserygutso is feeling pretty pleased with himself. He even kept the gardener on, because for some peculiar reason he doesn't even charge for his services.

All this draws me to the conclusion that if you want a long, happy, and harmonious relationship, the best way to achieve this is to spend as little time together as possible. If you want to make it to your diamond wedding anniversary, the answer is simple, live apart.

Chapter 21

Four Words That Scare Me To Death

S ome things scare me; sharks, snakes, people texting while they drive at 100 mph, mad axemen on the loose in my neighbourhood late at night, missing last orders at the bar. They all send the fear of God into me. But there's one thing that makes them pale in comparison. There's something far worse than venomous snakes, 15 m long Great Whites and missing your last pint on an evening. Just four little words, uttered by your loved one. Individually, the words are meaningless. However, when arranged in the correct order and spoken by your wife, girlfriend, partner—they become a nightmare of indescribable proportions. Those words? "We need to talk." Give me a moment, I need a stiff drink.

There are only three places these words are said to me.

1: In bed. I wake up in the morning, stretch, cough, and roll onto my side only to witness my wife staring at me, intently. She's clearly been awake a while, three hours or more, waiting, planning, imagining. She has a glint in her eye that I initially mistake for a "here I go, this is my lucky day." No, it's not my lucky day! If there was a 360° spectrum for amorous intentions, getting your leg over would be at 0° and the look in my wife's eye would be 180°. Then she says it. "We need to talk."

2. In the kitchen. I stagger downstairs gasping for a hot cup of tea and an intravenous drip of coffee which has been laced with paracetamol, ibuprofen and morphine. Yes, it was a big night, not that I can remember

much about it—apart from the police turning up at some point. God knows what all that was about?

My wife is unusually silent, which I count as a blessing—initially, due to my throbbing head. Then she says, "Do you remember what you did last night?"

I reply, "Of course, I do. I went to bed."

She responds (as in screams) with, "Before that!" As the caffeine slowly drips into my main artery I experience a few flashbacks. There was a woman with a rash and bad halitosis *(is there good halitosis? Ed)*. There was a very short man called "sawn-off" and I vaguely remember a prize-winning cucumber—after that, it's all a blank.

"Do you remember the woman with the rash?" my dearest asks.

"Yes."

"Do you remember the small man?"

"Yes—Sawn-Off was his nickname," I reply confidently.

"It wasn't his nickname until you called him that! And have you forgotten about the cucumber incident, shortly followed by the arrival of the police?" Hmm... okay, she's got me there. Then she says it, "We need to talk."

3. In the living room. This is the worst one of all. You know it's moved up a notch if the "we need to talk" has migrated to the living room. This is serious shit. It's a code red. A dozen Klaxons are now going off in my head. I feel the need to escape. I take a seat in the comfy chair. My wife takes a seat opposite, always very slowly, deliberately, like she's suddenly fallen into some slow-mo parallel universe. She shuffles forward to the edge of the cushion. Her elbows rest on her knees. Her hands are clasped together as though she's praying—either that or she's surreptitiously pulling the pin from a hand-grenade.

She looks at you the same way an experienced teacher looks at a recalcitrant naughty schoolboy—you know, severely disappointed, there's no hope for you, you're on the road to ruin, and she's over it all—that sort of look.

I feverishly rack my brain to figure out if I've done something I shouldn't have, or if I haven't done something I should have. I'm like a rabbit that has been chased down a fox hole. There's no way out! As she begins to speak I go deaf. Not deliberately, it's my subconscious kicking in, trying to save me from pain. My hands are clammy, my chest tightens, my breathing accelerates, my mind turns to gloop. Fight or flight pays me a visit, but I decide saying nothing is probably a good strategy until I find out what I've done—or haven't done.

A thought flashes across my mind. I've arranged to meet Steve, at 1:30 pm in The Firkin Frog to quaff a few pints of Cum Guzzlers Ruin before sitting down to watch the big footy game on satellite TV. The ill-conceived rendezvous is now in serious jeopardy.

She stops. She asks the other question, which is nearly as scary as, "we need to talk" but this time it's, "Well, what have you got to say for yourself?"

I reply with a limp, "Sorry".

She looks amazed, but not in a good way. "I'm sorry, but sorry doesn't cut the mustard anymore," she replies.

How come sorry still works for her but not for me, I think to myself. Possibly I'm only allowed so many "sorrys" throughout my life and I've burnt all mine up pretty quickly, whereas she's been holding hers in reserve.

Or possibly I'm a twat — unlikely, but a remote possibility. And more importantly, what type of person cuts mustard up? Is there a mustard cutters union I've never heard about? I decide not to mention the mustard, it will only end in tears and muddy the waters.

It turns out it wasn't just one thing, it never is. There was wet washing that had been sitting in a basket for 3 days that I should have hung out on the line. (God forbid! It's the end of the world as we know it. Hold the front page—"Felonious Fool Forgets To Hang Washing Out—The Final Straw! Invest In Gold Now And Head To The Hills!" Oh, and I was supposed to fix the fly screen in the bedroom. Give me a break! I've been meaning to do that for the last six years, another couple of days won't make a difference. And lastly, I'm spending too much time writing books that nobody reads. Okay, she's got me there, there's no comeback from that one —well, apart from this, which I said with a certain cocky aplomb (that I deeply regretted later).

"One day, my dearest, petal rose, you will be sipping on an Angel's Tit (calm down—it's a cocktail) whilst getting a massage from a twenty-seven-year-old Italian male model called Rock Hard, on the Mediterranean isle of "Afkmegently", all thanks to the money made from my "inane rambling scribbles" as you so eloquently describe my books. When that day arrives, you will turn to me and say—sorry. And being a man with a forgiving nature, plus many other commendable attributes—of which there are too many to list, I will say, apology accepted, let's move on."

I like to keep this newsletter mostly clean, so I cannot repeat what my wife's response was. Let's just say it's a phrase she doesn't use often, and I suspect is anatomically hard to achieve, unless, as a man, you are over-endowed in a certain department and are quite supple.

Chapter 22

The Gathering Storm

Well, well, well, it was only last month I was talking about the overuse of the word, "**unprecedented**" and as you will be painfully aware, we are now in "unprecedented" times of saying the word "unprecedented". Yes, it looks like the apocalypse is nearly upon us. It won't be long before hordes of zombies are roaming the streets and supermarkets buying up all the toilet rolls, they can find. After all, I can't think of anything worse than watching the impending Armageddon unfold without a fifty-year stockpile of Andrex 4-ply stashed safely in the vault. Forget about non-perishable food, medication, petrol, just hand over the bog roll buddy, otherwise, you're going to receive some ballistic therapy.

The other day I found myself in a less than salubrious part of town i.e. Dodgy Avenue. As I passed a litter-strewn alleyway, an unsavoury looking man approached me. He was unshaven, ill-kempt, and wore a long dirty overcoat. He flipped open one side of his coat. For one horrible moment, I thought he was a flasher, but it turned out he was far worse. He was a "dealer".

"Hey, mate," he said, "you interested in some special gear?" On the inside of his coat was stapled several sheets of toilet roll. "I can get as much as you want; 4-ply, 3-ply, 2-ply, what's your poison?"

"I'm sorry," I replied, "but I'm clean. I once had a bad experience with 2-ply and have never touched the stuff since. By the way, what's the cost?"

The price he quoted me was enough to buy a small car. I told him he was dreaming, but undeterred he flung open the other side of his coat.

"Okay, I can do you a special deal on this? It's hardcore and difficult to come by these days, but it will get you through the bad times." Pinned to his lining was a sheet of Izal. For those of you who are a bit longer in the tooth, you will probably remember this product. For those who are younger, let me explain.

Boffins invented Izal Medicated toilet roll a few million years ago. It had the absorbent qualities of marble and the texture of sandpaper (medium grit). I'm not sure why it was called "medicated" unless they meant you had to be under medication to use it. It was found in schools, hospitals, public inconveniences, and some friends homes whose parents were extremely frugal or had a warped sense of humour. I'm not sure who the first person was who thought using greaseproof paper to wipe your arse with was a good idea. His or her name appears to have been wiped from the history books, a lot more efficiently than Izal medicated could ever have managed.

The Romans had this one sussed long before a cute Labrador puppy came romping across our TV screens. They used an implement called a spongia to get that supreme clean feeling. A spongia was a sea sponge (deceased, I'm assuming) attached to a long stick and left in running water. When Claudius had finished his ablutions, the sponge was pushed through a hole in the toilet and, well, X marks the spot, I guess. You wouldn't want to march into battle against 10,000 blood-thirsty Gauls with a dirty bottom—would you? It could throw you right off your game.

Chapter 23

The Olympics

The Latin motto for the Olympics is "Dulce et Decorum Est." *(No, it's not—Ed)*. Which translated, means "Faster, Higher, Stronger TV Ratings." Why do I bring the Olympics up? Bloody good question, and a question I don't have an answer for. Oops, yes of course I do. It's March 2020 and the Olympics are to be held in Japan this coming July. I think the Olympic committee and the Japanese, could possibly be in denial about a nasty little bug doing the rounds at the moment. But as I've said before, you can lead a horse to water, but you can't pass a camel through the eye of a needle—well, I suppose technically you could if the needle was big enough and you had the inclination and a lot of time on your hands.

When I was a child, growing up, *(superfluous–all children grow up—Ed)* I loved the Olympic Games. For some reason, it was mostly held during the summer school holidays *(funny about that, being called the summer Olympics—Ed)*. Okay, Ed, I'm sorry, but I'm going to have to pick you up there. Summer does not occur during the same months the world over.

For example, in Britain, summer is supposed to be June, July and August. In reality, it usually occurs on the 27th of June and the 4th of August, whereupon we have a nice sunny day before it turns a little chilly in the evening. And that's it—summer's over until next year. In Australia, their summer begins in mid-October and runs through to early May. And it's never chilly, unless you call sub 30°C, chilly. I feel sorry for their other seasons. They have to cram Spring, Autumn and Winter into four short months. Anyway, who cares about Australia *(Australians? Ed)*. More people live in the next-door council estate than live in the Land Down Under. However, I digress—where was I? Ah, yes, the Olympics.

I loved watching track and field events. I could relate to them, after all, the Olympics were invented by the Greeks to replicate events on the battlefield. It was beneficial to run very fast over short distances. It was a bonus if you could jog at a steady pace over long distances. Being good at the javelin is obvious and I'm not even going to discuss the discus *(actually, that's quite good for you—Ed)*. But my favourite sport to watch was always the steeplechase. Now that is a sporting event, my friends.

The main reason I enjoyed it so much, was there would always be some hapless idiot who tripped over the steeple and face planted into the water. I remember me and my brother would roll around in hysterics on the carpet. The more they repeated the fall on TV, the funnier it would get.

But why was the steeplechase invented? I can only assume the Ancient Greek Olympic Committee, had a cruel sense of humour.

"Right, Achilles, what have we got?"

"Ahem... thank you, Gonnadios. For the track, we have the very short fast run, the medium run and the Marathon. In the field, we have the discus, the javelin, the hammer throw, synchronised swimming and needlework."

"Hmm, I think we need another event for the track. Any ideas?"

"Well, I have had one idea, but it's a bit silly."

"Don't be embarrassed, Achilles, what is it?"

"Well, we have another medium race but this time we litter the track with farm gates they have to jump over."

"Hmm... I like it."

"Wait, there's more. We have one especially large gate, and on the other side we have a long water pit."

"Ha-ha! You're such a heel, Achilles. But how do we sell it to the competitors?"

"We tell them they are being pursued by the Persians through a farmers field."

"Right, it's settled. And moving onto the last item on the agenda; submissions for new events. I believe we have one from Britannia. They have put forward something called cricket. Achilles, explain the rules to me."

"Of course, Gonnadios. You may want to grab a strong cup of coffee and some muscle relaxants before I begin."

Some events shouldn't be in the modern Olympics: football, rugby, cricket, tennis and of course my pet-hate—dressage.

For those of you who are unfamiliar with dressage, let me explain. Take a magnificent equine beast in the peak of physical fitness, sleek, shiny, honed, muscular. You put its hair in curlers *(it's called a mane—Ed)* and plait its tail, so it now looks like Pippi Longstocking. You put four white Bobbysocks on its feet, *(I think they're called hooves—Ed)* and give it a name like, "Anastasia Sugar Plum Fairy the III."

The majestic black stallion previously went under the name of "Black Stealth" and is non-too pleased with his new name. Once he sees his reflection in a mirror, you know there's trouble brewing.

Not content with humiliating the horse with the hairdo, effeminate name, and girly socks, they now rub salt into the wounds. They make him prance around like a female impersonator in stilettoes who is having a diva moment. Sugar Plum is made to walk backwards and sideways on tippy-toes and spin around like a model ballerina in a music box.

The only enjoyment, Black Stealth... sorry, Sugar Plum gets from it all is sniggering at the other horses who are all dressed similarly and the fact he's already decided in advance there's no way he's even going to attempt to jump the big gate with the puddle of water behind it. There's only one person going over that fence—and it's not him.

I'm not suggesting they remove dressage from the Olympic Games completely. I just think they should get rid of the horses. The riders should be made to do the silly walks, run around in circles, and try and jump two-metre-high fences, with razor wire on the top—to add a bit of spice. Now, that I would watch.

I think in a recent Olympics they introduced BMX, which I enjoyed watching. The only problem I had with it, was the competitors.

When I see someone on a BMX bike, I expect an acne-ridden fourteen-year-old, called "Razor", with his trousers resting below his buttocks, listening to skate punk on his cordless headphones, whilst making his way to the skate park to unload his stash of methamphetamines. But the BMX Olympians were nothing like that. They were all about thirty-years old and were called names like, Graham Braithwaite from Chipping Norton who works as an accountant at Price Waterhouse Coopers. Come on, if you're still dicking about on kiddie bikes at thirty, you need to take a damn hard look in the mirror. Mind you, if you're an accountant, you should have looked in that mirror a long time ago. However, I digress.

Now, as you know, I like to do a lot of intensive research before I throw my words out into the world—sometimes up to five minutes per newsletter. After all, if I wanted to spout ill-conceived, non-sensical, half-truths based on misinformation, prejudice, and the Gospel according to halfwits, I would have become a Shock Jock, a Social Commentator or run for parliament. But no, I follow due diligence and during my research, I noticed something interesting about the Olympics. Basically, we've dodged a bullet. I'm not sure how that's possible unless you are a Kung Fu actor, but nevertheless, I'll explain.

The fifth modern Olympiad (research) was held in Stockholm in 1912. Two years later the world was at war.

In 1936, Berlin was the Olympic host. Watching on, with great enthusiasm, was a madman with a bad haircut, a penchant for lederhosen and a severe case of black mould festering on his top lip. He was less than impressed with the German medal count and decided he would embark upon his own form of Olympics—which, to give him some credit, he did with great gusto. But ultimately, he dropped dead before the finishing line.

Two years after the Berlin Olympics, Hitler took control of Sudetenland (not to be confused with Sunderland which is in the NE corner of England —and I can assure you, no one would want to take control of that place— nor could they, even if they wanted). Shortly after, the world was at war again.

Keep up, keep up! The bombshell is coming *(awful choice of words— Ed)*.

Let's jump forward to the 30th Olympiad—held in Great Britain in 2012. If history repeats, as some say it does, the world should have been at war again in 2014. We are now a good six years past that deadline—so, you see the extrapolation? We dodged the bullet and learnt from our mistakes, *(did you consider leap years? Ed)*.

To finish, I guess my message is this; as humans, we can act bloody selfish and aggressive at times. The only way to combat this is to look back at history and learn from our mistakes and when we see similar patterns emerge, we must resist them. Here endeth the lesson.

Chapter 24

The Only Constant Is Change

A great saying, and one that I love—but it's not technically true. I think you'll find there are many constants in the world. For example, the speed of light, gravity, relativity, dickheads hoarding toilet roll, my jobs list the wife hands me each morning. Actually, that's a lie. The jobs list is not a constant. It's multiplying at an exponential rate. It's like a weird Quatermass experiment concocted in the kitchen by my wife. The last time I looked at it, I calculated I would need to live until I was at least 123 years old to complete it, not taking into account public holidays. I am blessed that my family's genes have longevity built into them, but we are not Time Lords or Vulcans, at least I don't think we are, although my Great Uncle Jeremiah Gotobed had exceedingly pointy ears. At least I think they were ears?

I always try to look on the bright side of life, and one good thing to come out of these "unprecedented" times, is I've found loads of new hiding places to escape being handed the dreaded list; the wardrobe, under the bed, in the shoebox outside and squatting in a long-abandoned cubby house built for my daughters. Actually, it was only built because it was once on a list.

I'm not a list sort of person. I can imagine Stalin and Mussolini being list makers.

"Hey, Benito, why do these damn trains never run on time? Can you sort it out?"

"No problem, I'll add it to my list. Right, where was I? Ah, yes; order 50,000 black coloured shirts from Hugo Boss, invade Greece and Ethiopia, round up the communists, send Adolf a jar of my homemade rhubarb jam, de-flea the cat and get the trains to run on time—sorted! Ooh! I almost forgot... get some new piano wire."

Lists seem to suck all the joy out of life, they snuff out spontaneity and lazing around, two attributes that come naturally to me. Sometimes, when I'm in the mood, I can spontaneously do nothing—it's a gift.

You've heard of serendipity, but have you heard of its antonym, zemblanity? *(You've made that up—Ed)*. Zemblanity means the ability to do something that turns out to be an unpleasant discovery that you should have expected. Like publishing a boxset of travel books at the start of a pandemic or re-mortgaging the house to invest in Holiday Park. It's called the Sadim touch (come on keep up—Midas backwards!!!).

When I'm not evading the list-maker I have been quite busy. I have updated several book covers—mainly the cover to Discombobulated— Keep On Keeping On. This cover originally had a large round blob of multi-coloured paint on the front of it, not dissimilar to a certain virus that is doing the rounds at the moment, proving that zemblanity can strike the best of us.

Chapter 25

Invicta Rome

During my self-imposed, forced hibernation, I have had a lot of time to think *(Oh no... this doesn't bode well—Ed)*. There's a hell of a lot of quotes that involve Rome and Romans.

One of the most famous is, "Friends, Romans, countrymen, lend me your ears." I'm not sure what was wrong with his own ears, but this was a eulogy given by the famous Welsh actor, Richard Burton, to Julius Caesar *(Mark Anthony, actually. At the funeral of Julius Caesar—Ed)*. The quote continues, "Ask not what your country can do for you, but what you can do for your country," which is very inspiring. *(Despite you crediting the wrong person by a distance of nearly 2000 years—Ed)*.

There's another famous saying I'm sure you've heard, "When in Rome do as the Romans do." It's a simple enough analogy to understand, i.e. when in a foreign place, adopt the customs and rituals of the locals. However, I find it a bit rich, coming from the Romans. If ever there was a race of people who didn't adhere to this premise, it was the bloody Romans! It should have read, "When anywhere, do as the Romans do and say, otherwise you'll end up with a gladius up your freckle." *(Hmm, you may want to clarify that a gladius is a sword and not a Roman Legionnaire—Ed)*.

Here's another phrase that I take issue with; "All roads lead to Rome." I put this to the test yesterday and set off on my daily walk along "Unprecedented Avenue". After four hours walking, I found myself at an open-cut coal mine, being lambasted by a man in a hard hat and a hi-viz vest. I told him I was looking for Rome and asked him if I was on the right road? I can't repeat what he said but security let me off with a warning and suggested I seek help.

I'll end by quoting this famous inscription, which was found etched into a wall in the ancient city of Pompeii, "Has someone left the gas on?" *(This is going to be a long, long lockdown—Ed)*.

Chapter 26

Motivation & Focus

B eing a writer is a solitary job, which is why I like it. Self-isolating for me is not an issue, I'm a seasoned professional. Although, with the "List-Maker" now in permanent residency, there have been a few adjustments I've had to make. Like waiting on her hand-and-foot because hers is a "proper" job whilst I'm just messing about on the keyboard writing "nonsense". This is hard to argue with, mainly because it's true.

Writing books is not easy, I'm not saying it's hard either, but you need two things; motivation and focus, focus, focus—and an imagination... plus a computer and certain word processing software... and an internet connection for research... and, well, I seem to have lost my train of thought. Ah, yes! Motivation and focus, focus, focus!

So, the other day, I decided that for twenty-four hours I would keep a small notebook and pencil on me at all times (apart from in the shower). My intent? To document the vast amounts of focus and motivation that is required to be a writer. I thought it may be beneficial to other people to understand and appreciate the immense sacrifices that writers make. I hope some of you will be inspired to become writers yourselves. By following my daily habits, it is achievable.

3:00 am

I awoke from a peculiar dream in which I was desperately searching for a toilet in an old people's retirement village. A man with a face like a battered Pavlova informed me that all toilets had been sequestrated by the Catholic Priesthood until further notice. He then began picking rhubarb.

I ponder the dream for a while trying to eke out the meaning from it... none is forthcoming.

3:15 am

Go to the toilet for a wee. Remind myself not to flush, as the water pump will start up and run for at least fifteen minutes and keep me awake.

3:18 am

Flush the toilet and curse myself for being a fuckwit!

3:30 am

Cannot get back to sleep as my mind wanders. It's not even as though I am having productive thoughts. So far, I've imagined the following; do fish have eyelids? If all of space and time is round, does it mean one day Voyager 1 will return to earth? I wonder if Mrs McCleggity has found her wedding ring yet? What does the inside of an atom look like? Did I shut the shed door?

4:30 am

Still wide awake and decide I may as well get up and start work on my next book. It will give me a three-hour head start over the List-Maker.

5:30 am

Really might as well get up, I'm achieving nothing laying here wondering what Maria Sharapova's favourite colour is or if Dustin Hoffman empties his own rubbish bins.

6:30 am

Right, definitely getting up now. That's three wasted hours. Promptly fall asleep.

7:30 am

Woken by the List-Maker asking me what I'm making for breakfast. Obviously, she's still suffering from that nasty bug that has rendered her arms and legs inoperable.

7:40 am

Make a coffee and head outside to sit on the deck and reflect on life. Decide to look at Facebook on my phone instead. Cats, cats, dogs, Trump, people falling over, people fighting, cats, Trump, cats, dogs, Jesus saves, Trump, people falling down holes, people singing—badly, cats, Trump, cats, fuck me... an elephant, people falling off roofs, cats.

7:55 am
Breakfast is done, and the dishwasher is making light work of the dishes, plates, and cutlery—well, I'm good at it. You know what they say— practice makes perfect.

8:07 am
About to head upstairs to begin work on my manuscript. But first, the List-Maker wants some help with a computer issue. It will be something devilishly fiendish like how to copy a file from one folder to another.

8:16 am
I'm sat in front of the screen with a blank word document staring back at me. Hmm... maybe, I'll have a quick check of Facebook and jump on the internet to catch up with the latest news.

8:17 am
Facebook; cats, Trump, cats, dogs, people cutting trees down with a chainsaw, cats, babies singing, dogs, Trump, people in road-rage incidents, cats, top tips on how to clean your oven, dogs, Trump... cats.

9:17 am
Decide to check my book sales dashboard to see how many books I've sold in the last 24 hours. Hmm, not bad... I've made £23.87 so far today. Decide to check my ad spend. Not a good idea! Ad spend—£49.59.

9:30 am
Staring at a blank screen again. I have an idea and am about to begin typing when the List-Maker calls up the stairs... again. She has a problem! Yeah, me too!

9:50 am

Connected the List-Maker's laptop to the upstairs printer. She's impressed with her new laptop as it comes with a drinks holder that she sits her coffee cup in. I explained to her it's the DVD tray.

10:20 am

Sat outside on the deck having a cup of tea and a cheese toastie, wondering if Rod Stewart ever washes his own underwear?

10:40 am

Decide to check my emails before beginning my new story. I constantly get emails from a company that is trying to sell me a mail-order bride from Swaziland! I highlight their latest email and am about to hit the delete button when the List-Maker calls up the stairs again—hmm, maybe I'm being a bit hasty on deleting the email. I'll put it in my secret folder named, "Secret".

11:03 am

The List-Maker fancies a cup of "proper" coffee from the coffee shop in town. Anything to get me out of the house! I'll take the dog with me as well and we can have a walk around the local park.

11:30 am

Walking around the local park wondering if Gordon Ramsay wears boxer shorts or is more of a Y fronts sort of man? I find a golf ball.

12:15 pm

Ordered the coffee and am now stood talking to some random woman about fly-fishing in Borneo... I'm not even sure how we got onto the subject. One minute we're chatting about the price of butter in Safeways, the next, we're discussing what's the best lures to catch a Bony-tongue fish.

12:30 pm

I've had too much caffeine and now have a splitting headache. The List-Maker wants me to format a training manual for her, which doesn't help with the headache. Decide to take a couple of paracetamol and drink copious amounts of water.

12:45 pm

Right, this is it, time to write. I have an idea! I begin typing:

"The..."

The List-Maker calls upstairs to inform me she's hungry and what am I making for lunch? A few things spring to mind; A BLT laced with cyanide or maybe cheese and crackers washed down with a nice chilled glass of liquid plutonium.

1:30 pm

Back in front of the screen again. What was my idea? It's escaped me now. I stare at my productivity for the day;

"The..."

Aha! Yes, I remember my idea. Right, here we go. I'll soon be in the zone then watch out baby! I'm about to type when my phone rings. It's from a complete stranger until I realise it's my daughter who I'd almost forgotten existed. She wants to know if I can pick her up from her boyfriend's place. I tell her I was in town half-an-hour ago and why hadn't she called me sooner? She informs me the battery on her crystal ball is flat. Smart-arse... I don't know who she gets it from.

1:50 pm

As we are driving back to Fortress Northouse, my daughter informs me my nasal hair is getting out of control. Nice...

2:15 pm

I'm in the bathroom staring up my nostrils. Hmm... it has gone a bit viral. Another week and I'd have a moustache like Adolf Hitler's. I decide a good trim is in order. I decide to do my ears and eyebrows at the same time. One must keep up appearances.

2:37 pm

Back at my desk. Motivation and focus, motivation and focus... they are the keys to success. First, I decide to check Facebook. Cats, cats, Trump, people falling off ladders, dogs, Trump... you get the picture.

2:50 pm

"The..."

Hmm, I'm not sure I like the opening, it could do with a complete rework. Before I get the chance to launch into it, the List-Maker has another computer issue. She wants to know which hole to stick her USB drive into. I resist the temptation to tell her exactly where to stick it, she'd probably comply.

3:12 pm

Tech disaster averted and I'm back at my keyboard. Now, where was I? A rework... no, I'll stick with what I've got. It's got a certain energy and urgency about it. Readers always like a good hook to suck them in.

"The..."

Here we go, stand back, Northouse is in the zone! My daughter pops her head around the door and asks if I can drop her at her boyfriend's? To be honest, I could do with getting out of the house for a while.

4:09 pm

I'm in the office staring out of my window wondering if Sting has ever changed a flat tyre?

4:26 pm

This is ridiculous! I've been awake since 3 am and all I have for my efforts is, "The..." I decide a chilled glass of pinot grigio will relax me and get the creative juices flowing.

4:45 pm

Maybe one more glass. I can feel a Tsunami of creativity is about to come crashing onto my shore any moment now!

5:27 pm

The bottle of wine has made me feel a little sleepy. A quick power-nap will help unleash my formidable writing powers.

5:30 pm

As I drift off, I wonder whether Mother Teresa ever played bingo?

6:15 pm

The List-Maker wakes me to ask what I have planned for dinner. "Russian Roulette" I reply once she's safely out of earshot... and to be honest with you... I don't care who fucking wins - either way, it would be a blessing in disguise!

8:30 pm

Dinner is finished, the pots are done, the dog is fed, the cat is ironed, everything is tickety-boo and ready to go for the next day. Pre-planning and being organised is essential to achieving things. Clear the decks, hoist the Jolly Roger and splice the mainbrace—the battlecruiser, HMS Northouse is about to set sail!

8:31 pm

I decide a little light relief would be beneficial before I return to my manuscript. A couple of episodes of Peaky Blinders should do the trick. Unfortunately, the List-Maker has already hogged the TV and is watching a re-run of the X-factor. Why anyone would want to watch it the first time around is beyond me!

8:45 pm

"The..."

Hmm, maybe I'll check the latest news headlines before I start.

8:47 pm

Bend me over and tickle my arse with a salted kipper! The government reckons this lockdown could last six months! I'm wondering if it's possible to be put into a medically-induced coma until the end of September...

9:05 pm

Only **4380** hours to go until the lockdown is over...

9:06 pm

Focus, focus, focus... writing is all about focus...

9:07 pm

"The..."

No point starting now, I'll get an early night and rise at the crack of dawn to begin afresh. A good night's sleep will unleash a writing frenzy never before witnessed by mankind. I'll check my book sales one last time before bed. Nice, £32.28 in sales today. And the ad spend? Sweet merciful crap with bells on! Why did I do that?

10:10 pm

Brushing my teeth extremely slowly, for some reason I can't explain. I've just realised I've spent the entire day under the misapprehension it was Tuesday—it wasn't, it's Thursday. What the *hell* happened to Wednesday? Maybe the government deleted it for reasons best known to themselves.

10:30 pm

Can hear the List-Maker cackling from downstairs. She's either watching a comedy or has been informed she'll be working from home for another 6 months.

11:59 pm

Lying in bed staring at the ceiling fan slowly spinning around. I count the revolutions for a good thirty minutes. 954, 955, 956, 957...

3:02 am

I wake from a horrendous nightmare! The word, "**The**" had grown legs and sprouted arms and was chasing me through the British Library throwing Jefferey Archer books at my head. It could have been worse, it could have been Jilly Cooper books.

3:10 am

I go to the toilet for a wee and remind myself not to flush.

3:11 am

I flush the toilet like the clueless knob-jockey that I am! Damn it!

3:15 am

Impossible to sleep now. The water pump kicks in and out, incessantly. It sounds like an asthmatic Clydesdale in an asbestos factory. My mind tries to solve the world's problems... again. I wonder if Robert De Nero has ever caught his willy in his zipper?

4:15 am

I may as well get up and start writing. I'll have a cup of coffee and check Facebook first, though. Then, the writing machine begins. It's not hard, it's all about focus, focus, focus. I idly ponder if Vladimir Putin has ever visited Cleethorpes in January?

The Lockdown Diary Blues

Book 3

Chapter 27

Ain't No Cure For The Lockdown Blues

Monday

It's early Monday morning and I've locked myself out of the house, (I'm a man of many hidden talents). Oh, the irony... locked out in lockdown and both self-imposed. It doesn't bode well for the forthcoming week. I phone the List-Maker, who is still asleep in bed. No answer. I grab a long pole from the shed and tap on the bedroom window. She eventually peers out, probably thinking she's having a nightmare—a bit-part in a crap comedy. I can't quite hear what she yells, but I can tell by her expression and hand gestures she's none too pleased. They say communication is 80% body language.

Wednesday

Pwwwwrrrppphhhp! That's the sound a horse makes as it vibrates its lips together. It's the sound I just made sitting in my office, staring at the garden. It's Sunday, all day, no... it's not, it's Wednesday, and it's barely over a week since I was sitting here gazing out of the window, wondering if Sting had ever changed a flat tyre. Well, guess what? I have a flat tyre—or at least a slow puncture. Where's bloody Sting when you need him? Probably walking on the moon or strolling through fields of barley, getting his allotted one-hour daily exercise. I've no idea what happened on Tuesday, and I really don't care.

Friday

I think I may have the early onset of senility. It seems I've misplaced yet another day. To misquote Oscar Wilde, "To lose one day may be regarded as a misfortune. To lose two looks like carelessness."

There's a hell of a ruckus coming from downstairs and eventually, I muster the courage to investigate. The List-Maker is in the kitchen, and it appears she's having a bit of a spring clean. These clear-outs happen on a regular five-yearly basis—she likes to keep on top of things. The sight that greets me resembles the opening battle scenes from "Saving Private Ryan".

"What are you doing?" I innocently (and foolishly—with hindsight) ask.

"I'm having a clear out! What does it bloody look like!" The kitchen bin is already overflowing with discarded packets, boxes, and tubs of food. I take a closer inspection.

"Why are you throwing all this out?" I innocently (and foolishly—with hindsight) ask. Some people never learn.

"Because!!!!! It's past its use-by date. Any more stupid questions?" Silly question—I have plenty, but I think *her* question may have been rhetorical. The List-Maker is a bit of a stickler for rules and regulations and sell-by-dates. I move closer to the bin and retrieve a tub of cottage cheese.

"What's wrong with this? I'm sure I only bought it a few weeks back?"

"Well, be my guest—you eat it," she replies. I spin the tub over and gaze at the sell-by-date—Dec 2016... hmm...

"You can't send this to landfill. You need to ring the council and ask them to send a Bio-Haz SWAT Team around to deal with it. If this gets into the water supply, it could wipe out a small city." I receive the death stare. I try to lighten proceedings. "Dec 2016, ha-ha, seems like yesterday. Doesn't time fly when you're having fun?" I say in a jocular manner. I receive a less than jocular response. Maybe it's time to change my flat tyre.

My jobs, let's call them chores, always follows a familiar path. They start off well, hit an obstacle, and nosedive into the abyss. The times I've changed hinges on a wonky door—the first five screws are removed with ease. The sixth—is threaded, or it has no head left. I have to resort to an electric drill, and when that doesn't work, a jackhammer.

Or the time I was building a fence. I put in 5 new fence posts. A breeze! My auger burrows down three feet into the earth as though drilling through pastry. Post number six is a different matter. The auger hits something hard, which turns out to be the northern tip of the continental shelf. Changing my tyre follows a similar plotline.

Wheel lugs loosened, spare tyre at the ready, car jacked up—simples! All I need to do is pull the tyre off, replace it with the spare, reattach the nuts and we're rock 'n' rolling.

Unfortunately, the car wheel has other ideas. It has become emotionally attached to the brake drum and isn't about to enter divorce proceedings anytime soon. I push and pull at the malevolent bastard for a good 20 minutes, to no avail. I employ a rubber mallet and knock the shit out of it —not a sausage! I find a long piece of timber and attack it from the rear, using a large metal hammer to whack the timber with—nothing.

Okay, time for Plan B—Google. Sure enough, Google comes to the rescue by pointing me to YouTube. One guy says to spray WD40 into the bolt holes and wait an hour—sounds like my sort of remedy—i.e. an easy fix and I can do sweet FA for 60 minutes. Another tip suggests sitting on the ground with one foot on either side of the tyre, and vigorously kick at it in alternating movements. Another recommends putting the car into reverse, then 1st gear and rocking it back and forth until the wheel comes loose. And lastly, there's a guy who built his own widget that you can use as a lever, with a jemmy, to prise the wheel off. It looks good but takes three days to build and you need a degree in metallurgy and mechanical engineering.

The wasted hour and WD40 didn't work. Nor did sitting on my arse in the driveway doing a Michael Flatley impression. And rocking the car back and forth was also fruitless. Time to phone a friend.

"... so, you've definitely tried the mallet? Have you tried sitting on your arse and kicking it? Hey, what about putting it in reverse and..."

"Bye."

There's nothing left but to admit defeat. I put the bolts back on, lower the car, and pump the tyre up. There's only one solution to this—I must take it to a professional—Tyre Power!

Three hours have now passed on what should have been a 20-minute job. Before I leave for the tyre place, I pop my head back through the door of the house. For reasons best known to herself, the List-Maker is now only dressed in her bra and knickers—I don't ask. I sometimes worry about her sanity. Food has multiplied at an exponential rate. It floods from countertops, tables, boxes, the settee. Even the dog, a normally relaxed if singularly idiotic creature, is lying on her bed with paws over her eyes. Hmm... time for my trip to the tyre professionals. I'll try to drag it out a little. No need to rush these things.

I park the car up at the tyre shop and head into the reception. I stand on the "X" sticky tape situated 1.5m from the counter and inform the female attendant I have a slow puncture. She informs me they can fix it straight away if I'm happy to wait. I am... as long as it takes... the longer the better.

Ahh, tradies... don't you love them? They rarely smile and seem to have a fatalistic take on life. They realise there's no such thing as a simple job. Every task is fraught with problems and takes longer than envisaged. The bigger the problem, the more it costs.

The mechanic asks me which one it is. I tell him it's the Subaru. He looks at me like I'm a half-wit.

"Nah, mate, which tyre?"

"Oh, front, driver's side," I reply. He jumps into the car and drives it into the workshop. He hops out and inspects the tyres. He gives me the tradies stare, you know, the one which says, "Fuck me, you really are a clueless dumbbell, aren't you?"

"Not much left in these, mate! You're barely legal! You're down to the wire." He mournfully explains, referring to the tread on my tyres.

"Yeah, been meaning to get around to it. Anyway, my horoscope said not to plan any long trips for the next 6 months, so there's no point changing them yet." He stares back at me, a bit like the List-Maker did when I mentioned the cottage cheese and Bio-Haz.

I love "Schadenfreude", i.e. pleasure derived from someone else's misfortune. I am now happily leaning on a post, waiting for the moment the mechanic can't get the tyre off. Serves him right for being a condescending dickhead. It will be a fight to the death and my money's on the recalcitrant wheel.

He loosens the wheel nuts, positions the jack, then pumps the lever. The car slowly rises as he removes the nuts. Here we go! Time for a bit of free fun. He slaps the wheel with both palms, and it wobbles off onto the concrete, almost apologetically! The day is going from bad to worse.

While paying the bill, I ask the woman for a quote on 4 new tyres.

"I can do you four Michelins for £120—fitted," she replies. I'm pleasantly surprised.

"That's not bad—£30 each," I say. Now she gives me the "half-wit" stare.

"No! £120, each, plus £20 for wheel alignment." My nose begins to bleed.

⋙ ⋘

As I'm in town, I decide to pay a visit to Aldi's to pick up some provisions. I drive into the car park and immediately drive back out. The place is swarming with the walking dead, all with trolleys laden to the point of buckling the wheels. What's wrong with the world! There are no shortages! Well, at least there wasn't until these panic-merchants decided they needed enough toilet roll and flour to survive a nuclear winter.

Driving back to Fortress Northouse, I idly wonder if the Queen is a toilet roll or a bidet sort of person? The thought conjures up unpleasant imagery, and I soon push it to the back of my mind.

Back home, I poke my head through the door. The List-Maker is sitting on the couch, now dressed in her "activewear" actively doing fuck all! It appears the liberation of the kitchen stalled on the beaches of Normandy due to heavy resistance from the dried pasta and baked beans, the elite SS battalion of the non-perishable food world. I enter the house... tentatively.

"How d'you go?" she asks as she munches on half-a-cows arse stuck between two bread vans.

"Erm... yeah.... good. The guy says my tyres need replacing."

"How much?"

"Five hundred."

"Well, you need to get them sorted as soon as possible."

"No bloody way!" I respond.

"Why? What is wrong with you? When it comes to safety, there should be no scrimping!"

"Listen, I could be dead in a matter of weeks, thanks to this bloody virus. Imagine my distress knowing I'd forked out £500 on new tyres which will never be used!"

"You tight Yorkshire git! By the way, we have a rat!" Just when I think things can't get any worse... they get worse. I retire to my shed for a comforting glass or five of Cardboard Chardonnay.

Saturday

After all these years, I now understand how Bill Murray felt in Groundhog Day. At least he got to spend his time with Andie MacDowell. I can think of worse ways to spend my days... and nights. My body clock is all over the place, like a mad woman's shite. I tell the List-Maker I'm going to bed.

"But it's only 8 o'clock?" she replies in disbelief, as though I've just told her the dog has exploded.

"Yeah, I know. It is a bit late. Sleep is my only sanctuary."

I wake at 4:30 am. I idly wonder if Kate Middleton has ever played darts... probably not. I can't imagine her in The Hairy Badger shouting out, "One-hundred-and-eighty!" May as well get up and look at cats on Facebook. I could even get to work on my new book. I've doubled my word count in the last week. I now have two words, "The man...". Which man? And what's he going to do or say? Questions that remain unanswered. I blow air out through my mouth like a horse vibrating its lips.

Chapter 28

The Importance Of Being Idle

Sunday

I can hardly believe seven days have passed since my last newsletter. Apparently so! I could swear this has been a three-day week. This is bizarre because a week now feels like a month but time, events, meaninglessness, have all merged into one big gloopy splat, and although a week appears longer there is no demarcation of days and hours anymore.

I used to look forward to a Friday night when I could get smashed. Now it's every night. On Sunday's I eagerly anticipated church—the church of doing as little as possible and indulging in things that gave me pleasure. Monday morning would raise its weary head, and I had to deal with the unwelcome thought of work. Monday night was netball practise for my daughter, as was Tuesday, Wednesday, and Thursday, followed by the game on Saturday. And now... tumbleweed and crickets. I'm beginning to feel like Robinson Crusoe—I've even started to look like him, and he was fictitious!

Monday

It gets worse. Not only is the List-Maker "working from home", but school has resumed—from home. We are on a copper wire internet connection, which is moribund at the best of times. Well, today for me at least, it has ground to a halt. It would be quicker to employ carrier pigeons.

I know the culprit—my daughter—she's a compulsive streamer. She's supposed to be doing schoolwork online, but I suspect those "very efficient

& tech-savvy" teachers at her school won't have anything ready to go. They'll all be in the staff room smoking pot and infecting each other.

I believe my daughter is using her phone to watch reruns of Glee, Katy Perry in concert or what Kim Kardashian is having for breakfast.

"For God's sake! I'm trying to work here! I can't even get Google up... stop bloody streaming!" I yell. An unwarranted barrage of abuse from my daughter and the List-Maker, heads my way.It goes something like—"I'm an essential worker—I need the internet!" from the List-Maker. And "I'm studying here! This is year 11—it's a critical year! You get off the bloody internet!" from my daughter.

The List-Maker again, "All you're doing is writing stupid bloody books. There's a list of jobs for you on the table, why don't you try actioning some of those?" Hmm... actioning? A strange word to use in one's home. The List-Maker is increasingly speaking like a middle-manager. I see trouble ahead. Why did I open my big gob? I walked right into that one. I retire to the shed for a quiet glass of chilled white wine—well, it is past 2:30 pm, and there's a predicament to ponder. The only way for me to get anything done is to work when they're both asleep. Which means through the night. Considering my change in sleeping habits, this shouldn't be a problem. Sometimes I get up before I've even gone to bed... if that's possible... which it is... because I've done it.

Tuesday

I noticed in the online news, British MPs voted to give themselves an extra £10,000 as a subsidy for working from home. They never miss a trick, do they? What does "working from home" actually entail?

It means rising at 8:55 am and booting up your laptop so it looks like you're online by 9 am. Next comes a leisurely 1-hour breakfast as you watch dogs tap-dancing on Facebook. At 10 am you send an email to the "team" about your previous day's productivity—which is the greatest work of fiction since F. Scott Fitzgerald picked up his pen and sat down to write

The Great Gatsby. Next comes Netflix and binge-watching the first season of Peaky Blinders, followed by a leisurely lunch. At 1:30 pm you send your boss an email about a problem you've encountered. It's a fictitious problem you deliberately invented, about a project which doesn't exist, to make it appear you're busy. The boss, who was happily binge-watching "Little House on The Prairie", is straight onto the matter. Much to your great surprise, he replies, saying he's encountered the same issue. He says he'll look into it once he finds the time. Of course, he's hoping you'll forget about the fictitious problem about the project which doesn't exist, then everyone can get back to doing what they do best—i.e. fuck all!

Between 3:15 and 4:00 pm, you take your regular afternoon nap. Stuffing your face and staring at the television for five hours straight can be quite exhausting. At 4:55 pm you send your last email of the day, telling everyone you're completely snowed under. You ask the boss whether it's possible to do a few hours overtime each day and possibly some weekend work to catch up otherwise, the "wheels could fall off!" The boss agrees and says he's thinking of taking on extra staff to cope with the workload, which has grown exponentially since everyone vacated the office and began working from home. At 5:01 pm you crack open your first bottle of Pinot Grigio for the day and congratulate yourself on keeping the faltering economy from going into cardiac arrest.

Tuwednesday

I've completely ditched the opening to my new book and started afresh... I was getting bogged down, somewhat. I once read somewhere, the first 10 pages of a book are the most important. It must be action-packed or full of emotion, or preferably both. This way you suck the reader in, like dangling bait in front of a fish. After the first 10 pages you can pad the book out with 300 pages of complete dross, and it doesn't matter. Furthermore, the first 3 sentences are the linchpin to those opening "grab 'em" pages.

With this in mind, I set about my book with renewed vigour and impetus. After three hours of intensive creative thinking, which left me with a migraine, I had my opening gambit. It's high octane, emotionally charged... it's electricity; zap, pow, kaboom! Grab 'em by the balls! And here it is, a foretaste of what's to come. Read it and weep—Mr Hemingway!

"Reginald Bracegirdle lifted himself wearily out of bed. He put his tartan slippers on and shuffled unsteadily towards the toilet as fast as his brittle, arthritic legs would carry him. He desperately hoped his Marks & Spencer Y fronts wouldn't fall down before he reached his destination."

That, my friend, is what they call, literary napalm! You read it here first; I've coined the phrase. It will go viral once I've sent it out to my 12 newsletter subscribers, then it will be as ubiquitous as "unprecedented" or "once in a hundred-year event" or "actionable" (I have a long memory). It could do with a little touch-up here and there, but the unbridled essence of power and energy is undeniable. Only another 80,000 words of drivel to go.

I have two titles for my book and haven't yet decided on the best one. It needs to sum up the genre, storyline, POV. In essence, it needs to be powerful and grab the eye and the heart! The first title is,'Smoking Gun... For Hire!' The second one is, 'Don't Suck a Werther's Original While Lying on Your Back'.

The first one is punchy, the latter, more like a government health warning, which in these times, and with my readership demographic, may be more successful. I need to sleep on it.

Thursday... (maybe?)

I've spent the last hour staring out of my window thinking about nothing, which is quite an effort, but I am getting better at it. I idly wonder if Stephen King has ever been kayaking along the Leeds and Liverpool canal during a rainy bank holiday weekend?

Since lockdown began. I've been growing a beard... well, at least my face has. No, I'm not deliberately going for the hipster look—I'm an idle bastard and personal grooming has gone right out of the window, plus there is an ulterior motive.

I pick my daughter up from her boyfriend's parents' place. As she gets into the car, she lets out a piercing scream.

"No! Just no! What is that?"

"What's what?" I innocently ask.

"The fungus on your face? OMG! Have you got it? Is it one of the symptoms?"

"It's called a beard, sweet pea. A lot of men, and your Aunt Mary, have one. I think I resemble Brad Pitt—quite debonair!"

"I don't even know what that word means or who Pratt Bid is, but if you think you look 'cool', well, let me tell you—you don't! Get rid of it! You look like a cross between Shaggy from Scooby-Doo and the homeless man who loiters outside the public toilets near the park!" Ah yes, the sweet smell of victory. I knew it would annoy her—mission accomplished, despite the beard driving me crazy with the itchiness.

Thufrisatday

I wake in a cold sweat, which is hard to do when you're steaming hot. What a nightmare! I dreamt the tea harvest in India was about to get underway... but... they didn't have any workers to pick the crop because they'd all been sent to Antarctica to harvest krill and change the tyre on Jeremy Clarkson's BMW—don't ask—it's a dream. The upshot is there's a tea shortage! My God! I can live without coffee, toilet roll, flour, even sex... but not tea! My breathing becomes erratic. I switch the bedside lamp on and glance at the clock—4:30 am—funny about that. I begin deep breathing exercises and positive affirmations, which I learnt from a Gordon Ramsay cookbook.

"Calm, calm, calm, calm. The world is beautiful, I am beautiful, only positive energy may enter." After 20 minutes of Gordon's deep breathing exercises, learning a few new swear words, and having an idea for a Hispanic twist on Shepherd's Pie, I begin to relax. Phew! Just a nightmare, Simon, just a nightmare. Now sleep, my pretty one, sleep.

Nextday

By the time I come down the stairs in the morning, the List-Maker is already sitting in her favourite spot on the couch, watching the morning news. If she spends any more time on the couch, it will need to be surgically removed at some point. I think the fabric of the cushion has morphed with the DNA of her arse cheeks.

"What's the latest?" I ask, yawning as I put the kettle on.

"Not much. The USA is not going well, nor is the UK. Holland and Germany... hmm... not so good. Indonesia... stuffed. And Russia is finally admitting it's up shit creek without a paddle. Oh, and the tea harvest in India has been postponed."

"Noooooooooooooooo!!!!!!!!!"

I never thought it would come to this, but—it has come to this. Every time I now make a cup of tea there is a certain procedure to be followed. I even have a printout pinned next to the kettle. It reads, 'One tea bag in cup. Let stew for five minutes. Remove tea bag and place in "used-tea bag" plastic container. 8 pm each night, cut the bottom off tea bags and empty contents into a snap-lock bag. Freeze (in the freezer). Anyone not following these rules will be only allocated one sheet of toilet roll per day. Yours, in all seriousness, the Master of The House.' Next to it, someone has scribbled—'Dickhead!!!' I'm not sure 3 exclamation marks are warranted!!! Underneath, someone else has written 'He's such a knob—isn't he?' followed by another scribble, which reads, 'Yes!'

I recognise both near-illegible scrawls and because of my Poirot-like powers of deduction and rapier-like intuition; I know who the culprits are.

Plus, there's only been two other people in the house for over a month.

Someday

I've been listening to a lot of music lately, far more than usual. It brings me comfort, solace, and if I turn the volume up high enough, it drowns out the incessant calling from the List-Maker and her daughter for help with the fucking internet!!! I cannot control download speeds!

My daughter sends me an email attachment to print out as she can't connect to the home printer. The List-Maker 'scans-to-email' some documents and sends them to my email address so I can forward them to her email address.

I receive a text message from the List-Maker, who is in the downstairs room, asking if "quietest" is a word.

My daughter calls me on the phone asking how to "screenshot" her computer screen. She's in her bedroom, three feet away. Even Gandhi would have hit the bottle by now—his drinking partner—Mother Teresa! Talking of which, it's past 2 pm. Time for a little slug of Pinot Grigio—one bottle should suffice until the sun goes down—then I'll really hook into it.

A famous man once said, "............" ...damn it! I've forgotten what I was going to say. It was going to be something deep and meaningful. That's what too much pinet... pinto... pinot greg... greeayso, gregio, grigio—sod it... time for bed—it's well past 6:30 pm, after all.

Friday

I put my coat on and open the door. The List-Maker spots me making my escape for freedom.

"Where are you going? You're only allowed out for essential reasons; food, healthcare, exercise and essential work!"

"Don't stress. I'm just going in the back garden to set some traps."

"Traps? What sort of traps?"

"Carrier pigeon, sort of traps. After which, I'm going to be incognito for a while—I'm visiting four different supermarkets."

"What for? We have plenty to keep us going."

"Tea," I reply, almost ashamed—but not quite.

"No... don't tell me... you're going to the dark side; you're going to become one of them!"

"Yes, it's true, I'm going to become... a hoarder... a teabag hoarder. I'm not proud of the fact, but this has now got serious."

Newday

Another new day and I'm feeling in better spirits, mainly because I have 23 boxes of Yorkshire Tea stockpiled in the cupboards. My daughter is in the kitchen and is in an unusually good mood, which I find disquieting.

"Morning dad," she smiles at me as she flicks the kettle on.

"Morning," I reply, suspiciously. I can sense an imminent, coordinated dawn raid on my wallet.

"You know what," she continues, staring at my face. "I quite like your beard now. It suits you. Makes you look sort of... well, you know, cool." I push my wallet further down into my pocket.

"How much do you want and what for?" I ask, deciding attack is the best form of defence.

"Money? I don't need anything. I'm fine. All good. I realise times are tough and you make *absolutely nothing* from your writing." Not sure why she had to emphasise the words "absolutely nothing," but I let it pass. I move tentatively towards the kitchen cupboard. "Oh, you know the story about the tea shortage in India... well, guess what? Fake news." As I open the cupboard door, 23 boxes of Yorkshire Tea tumble down onto my head.

I'm in the bathroom staring into the mirror, admiring my beard. It's true, I do look cool. I've matured from a young-looking Brad Pitt into the more sophisticated George Clooney. But now it's time to shave the damn thing off—it's been driving me insane. If the only person it's now annoying is me, then it's time for it to go.

Clean-shaven and itch-free, I make my way downstairs. My daughter smiles at me.

"Sucker," she giggles. "I knew it would work." Damn it! This lockdown is like my own personal Kryptonite. I've been outwitted by a sixteen-year-old! Lift your game Northouse, otherwise, you're going downtown!

Chapter 29

Reasons To Be Cheerful

Monday
   In these times of boredom and apathy, it's important more than ever to keep one's mind active, stimulated, and razor-sharp. It would be easy to throw the towel in and succumb to cooking shows, reality TV and arguing with the fridge door. Before you know it, you break your day up with longer and longer snoozes and drinking in the early afternoon—not good habits to form.

Therefore, I've been proactive. Having always had an inquisitive mind and up for a mental challenge, I signed up online to receive a daily quiz. I've just received the first one in my inbox and I am sitting down with a cup of tea to get stuck into it. I've got to say, I'm feeling quite excited—oh, the simple things in life. Here we go!

"The Rimmington Express departs Upper Wanxoffen Station at 6:04 am. It travels at an average speed of 103 mph for a distance of 28 miles before entering Floppy-In-The-Hole Station, where it idles for 3 minutes. It picks up Eric Bland, a former calliper salesman from Dewsbury, before resuming the journey, this time with an average speed of 87 mph. It travels a further 64 miles before reaching its destination, Bottomley Overflow, where Eric is reunited with his vivacious and overly energetic girlfriend, Chlamydia Spreader. What time did Eric get out of bed?"

I hate these, "a train sets off at blah, blah, blah," sort of questions. They're always way too hard. Maths and timekeeping were never my forte.

Okay, this next one is more my sort of thing. It involves lateral thinking, something I pride myself on.

"If Sarah is married to Gary, and Steve is married to Kevin, and Gary's stepdad is the biological father of Kevin and is also having a torrid and illicit affair with Sarah's mother, who used to be a nun until she got drunk one night then who is the sister of Jerry?"

WTF! Where the hell does Jerry come into the picture? Which blithering idiot put this quiz together! Obviously, an insane asylum somewhere is missing a patron. Right, time for a glass of wine, followed by a snooze.

Tuesday

My disposition is a little delicate this morning and I'm looking forward to a strong cup of coffee and a piece of toast smeared with marmalade, hopefully in relative peace. Unfortunately, at 8:59 am my daughter arrives on the scene.

'You're supposed to be starting your online schooling in one minute,' I inform her.

'Don't worry, I've logged on already, so they think I'm there. Suckers.' It didn't take her long to figure that one out. If she were a couple of years older, she would make a perfect "stay at home worker". However, my desire for peace and solitude is but a fleeting dream. In one of the most cack-handed acts of gormlessness I've ever witnessed, my daughter jettisons the entire contents of the top cupboard onto the floor... a floor I mopped only yesterday. To her credit, she managed this unlikely feat with little effort. Sugar, flour, cocoa powder, hundreds and thousands, now cover the kitchen floor. It resembles a battleground in a patisserie between two irate and irrational pastry chefs. Just what my shattered nerves needed. There now ensues a blistering row.

"How in all of holy fuckdom did you manage that?" I yell. It wasn't really a question, more of an accusation. "People could practise for years and never pull that off!"

"It wasn't my fault!" she screams back.

"Oh, I see, maybe it was the work of our resident poltergeist? Or perhaps overnight we were invaded by an army of malevolent pixies? Of course, it was your fault!" The shouting and swearing from both parties reach a crescendo... until... the List-Maker makes an appearance to mollify the situation, in her usual manner, by throwing oil onto the fire, a tactic she is highly skilled in.

"What the hell is going on in here! I was on a video conference call with the team! It was bloody embarrassing! I had to tell them the effing and jeffing was coming from the television and mute the microphone on my laptop."

Everything soon calms down when my wife and daughter conclude the farcical mishap was all my fault. How silly of me. In hindsight, it was blindingly obvious. I didn't really want to nibble on my toast in blissful silence, no, instead, I wanted to roll around in cocoa powder and flour, for a laugh. Now is a good time to take my daily constitutional walk around the park before my head explodes.

Wednesday

My daily walk has now become somewhat hampered after a suggestion (read, insistence) from the List-Maker, I take the dog with me. Even at the best of times, the animal had minimal intelligence. It would have been easier to teach a slug how to change the oil on a combine-harvester than teach the mutt how to sit. However, she's now ancient, slightly deaf, partially blind and moves at the speed of a glacier on Valium.

Previously, my brisk walk around the park would take a bracing forty minutes, after which, I would feel refreshed and invigorated. It now takes a laborious sixty-five minutes, and we only get about fifteen feet from the car. For the first ten minutes, the dog stands on the grass looking bewildered, wondering where the couch has gone and what's happened to her dog bowl. I walk one way, she the other. I try calling her, but she either can't hear me, or she's reached the stage all old people eventually reach; the "I don't give a flying fuck anymore. I'll do what I want, not what you want." My mother and a couple of aunties are already at this stage. Actually, the List-Maker isn't far behind them.

Thursday

I'm sitting in my office gazing out of the window. I've stalled again. Yep, you guessed it—book trouble. I have serious doubts about my main protagonist—Roger Bracegirdle, an eighty-year-old, slightly incontinent, former chartered accountant who is now working undercover for Mossad. He hasn't the energy to make a cup of tea, never mind hunt down Nazis in the Bolivian rainforest. As for parachuting from the back of a Chinook helicopter, clutching a machine gun, rocket launcher and his incontinence bag—well, there's something, which doesn't quite ring true about the scene. It could be the name—Roger. I need something more dynamic like Darren, Trevor, or Kevin. I'll sleep on it.

Friday

The kitchen is a bombsite. Why someone can't clean up the night before, is beyond me. Wait, a minute... I cleaned up last night before I went to bed at 5:30 pm. If the kitchen had legs, it would have upped and left this house of insanity a few weeks back.

It used to live a fairly simple life. It was busy at breakfast time, encountered mild traffic at lunchtime and moderate traffic at dinner time. Apart from the occasional visit during the day, from the incumbents of the house, to make a cup of tea or coffee—that was it. Now it resembles the departure lounge at Heathrow Airport (before the bloody virus arrived).

I make my breakfast and clean up. My daughter appears and in her little girl voice asks me,

"Daaaaaad, will you make me pancakes?" Considering her slapstick buffoonery with the cupboard from a few days ago, I decide making pancakes may be the lesser of two evils. When she's finished, I clean up—again. Just as I'm about to head to my office to write, the List-Maker arrives on the scene. Her hair is done, there's a smattering of makeup on her face and she's wearing a smart business-like blouse. On the bottom half... she's in her knickers. Standards are slipping. I'm hoping the camera on her laptop malfunctions and pivots downwards during a video conference call. A little comic relief always lifts my day.

"Any chance you could make me a cheese omelette with Buffalo mozzarella and a side dish of steamed, lemon-infused greens to go with it?"

"Yes, of course. I do apologise, madam. Room service didn't pass your breakfast request on otherwise, I would have prepared it earlier." I cook and clean up again. An increasingly familiar scenario plays out for lunch and dinner. When all this is over, I reckon I could get a job in Marco Pierre White's Michelin star restaurant. This gives me another idea... I could put Roger Bracegirdle on the backburner and write a cookbook!

The "Lockdown Recipes—How to Eat Healthily and Avoid Murdering Your Family (plus bonus material: the dark art of sharing kitchen duties and other laugh-out-loud and highly improbable scenarios)".

Saturday

At last peace and tranquillity. My daughter is at her boyfriend's parents' place, and the List-Maker has gone for an hour's long walk with her friend along the river. I do hope neither of them falls in.

The List-Maker is on a fitness kick at the moment. Keto diet and exercise. Last week it was Weight Watchers and yoga. The week before, it was the "gorge yourself to death" and watch endless re-runs of Downton fucking Abbey, diet! I idly wonder what regime it will be next week. Vegetarian Keto, perhaps? Just to make my life, as chief cook and bottle washer a little easier. Anyway, I have a good hour to myself—time for some internet fun.

Damn it! The internet's down, some idiot at the telco has obviously forgotten to change the batteries. After an hour of staring at my blank diary, the internet is back up. Right, here we go, "MILFs Go Dogging on Kirrin Island"—here I come—pardon the pun. Oh no, I spot the List-Maker coming down the driveway with my daughter in the passenger seat. It never rains but pours—give me a break—at least once in a while!

It's 2:30 pm and I'm wondering whether it's too early to indulge in a glass of cheap white wine? What the hell! They put the clocks back last week, so it's really 3:30 pm or is it 1:30 pm? I can never figure it out. I'm not even sure why they bother with the archaic practice. Something to do with the cows, apparently. I didn't even know cows could tell the time. They must be brighter than they look... I struggle to know which day it is.

A ridiculous Facebook post, from my dim-witted brother, distracts me. He's been staring out of his window at a pigeon for over an hour; the fuckwit. In a lightbulb moment, he asks me this question:

"Why do pigeons have eyes on the side of their head instead of at the front?"

My reply, "Why not ask the pigeon? From one bird brain to another." I suggest he invite it inside for a game of scrabble. If I were a betting man, I know who I'd be placing my money on.

Right, it's a late night for me, 6:30 pm, and I'm away to bed. Or is it really 7:30 pm?

I wake from yet another terrible dream, in which I was stripped naked, rolled in treacle, flour, cocoa powder, and hundreds and thousands. A flock of giant pigeons, which have an uncanny resemblance to my brother, surround me. The pigeons are not easy on the eye, rather like my brother. They throw scrabble tiles at me, or to be more precise, high-value scrabble tiles; a Q, an X, a J, the odd Y and one blank tile. I try desperately to form a word as a cow holds a countdown timer in front of me. The only word I can form is "Joy". Which, as it turns out, I can place on a triple letter square and gives me a great score of 29. Stick that in your beaks and smoke it!

Tossing and turning for another hour, my mind all aquiver, I idly wonder if Hillary Clinton ever cleans her own shower? I can't imagine Bill getting out the shower spray and scrubbing pad.

I really must stop watching the ceiling fan spin around—it's becoming another bad habit. It's 4:30 am, I may as well get up and clean the kitchen before the hotel guests wake up and another day begins. Fuck you—2020!

Chapter 30

As Simple As This

Monday

I'm sitting outside having my early morning coffee or three before my daughter and the List-Maker wake up. Oh, peace and tranquillity—how blessed are thee. I receive a call from a number I don't recognise.

"Hello?" I answer.

"I hope you don't mind, but can you tell me who shot Liberty Vallance?" An unusual question at the best of times, but especially so for a Monday morning at 6:30 am. It sounds like an elderly woman and I should have hung up straight away but ponder the question... I like a challenge.

"Was it Jimmy Stewart or John Wayne? Hang on... maybe it was Gene Pitney?"

"I don't think the bus takes that route on a Sunday?" she replies. WTF!

"Okay, not a problem. Can you call me back in about two hundred years and I'll have a definitive answer for you?" I respond.

"Yes dear, I've got to hang up now as I need to take the giraffe out of the microwave... the buzzer has gone off!" The line goes dead. What a start to another week! This doesn't bode well.

It's ridiculous! The number of cups, glasses, plates, and cutlery we get through is driving me insane. I clean the kitchen about three times per day, but it doesn't matter what I do, dirty dishes still accumulate like some malevolent self-propagating crockery monster. It's like the Sorcerer's Apprentice scene from Fantasia.

Why am I doing so much clothes washing? No one has been anywhere, why are they going through so many clothes and towels? I've been back and forth to the washing line so many times, Google maps have it listed as a significant place of interest on my timeline.

Tuesday

The List-Maker has a new job, or should I say she is transitioning across to a new job. So, she now has two laptops, three mobile phones and more usernames and passwords than you can point a shitty stick at. My life has just become a lot harder. As she unpacks her new laptop, she marvels at a small piece of black plastic about 6" x 4" in size. It has a power cord connected to it.

"Ooh, look at this! I think it's a tiny printer, isn't that clever?" she stares in obvious glee.

"It's a docking station," I inform her, wondering who conducted the interview for her new job.

"A what station?"

"Docking. You place your laptop on it, and it automatically connects to your monitor, keyboard and mouse, plus any other gadgets you've got hooked up."

She laughs. "Well, I never! What will they think of next? What's for breakfast?"

"Poison toadstools on toasted rye?"

"Yummy, sounds great."

Wednesday

Never happened. Days keep disappearing. Wednesday obviously had better things to do than sit around all day as a placeholder. Can't say I blame it.

Thursday

I have an idea for a new book series: "Nigel Crowther Does Monte Carlo". It's going to be a rom-com, vigilante, thriller, sci-fi, clean Christianerotica, family saga, cosy cat mystery, with a steampunk elderly detective as the main protagonist. I'm planning a two-book trilogy aimed at people aged over 105 (my perfect demographic). It is set in Monte Carlo, Tierra del Fuego, and Cleckheaton. I can smell success... or is it the dog again?

Friday

Things go from bad to worse, to worser, to worserest. It's time to act. Drastic times call for drastic measures and there's nothing left for it. Yep, it's come to this—I call a family meeting!

My wife and daughter are sitting around the table as I stand in front of the fireplace with my thumbs tucked behind my braces as I rock back and forth.

"As CEO of the company, I've taken the unprecedented step of calling this Extraordinary General Meeting of Northouse Enterprises to address some pressing issues. I won't beat about the bush, the fact-of-the-matter is this—we are slowly sinking!" It's a grand opening sentence, on par with some of the greatest orators the world has known.

"Oh no," says the List-Maker, "it's not the subsidence issue in the corner of the house again, is it?"

"No! I'm speaking meteorically! And may I remind you the floor is mine at the moment, so please, silence—until I've finished. There will be a question-and-answer session at the end... followed by a 30-minute PowerPoint presentation. Therefore, I would appreciate everyone's undivided attention."

My daughter yawns as she looks at her phone. The List-Maker grabs a pen and notepad, and I know she's not taking notes of my speech—but building another bloody list—for me! The dog curls up in her bed and licks its vagina. "Okay, now I have everyone's attention—I'll begin. The curve has spiked! This morning I spent ten minutes with the dishwasher... it was on top of the shed roof ready to throw itself off! It was at breaking point. Luckily, I talked it down. The washing machine is also under the pump. Yesterday, I caught it with 5 litres of disinfectant, ready to ingest. If I had been a few minutes later entering the laundry, you realise what the consequences would have been?"

"It would have protected itself from getting Coronavirus?" quizzes my daughter unhelpfully.

"That's not even funny. Don't listen to silly old men—sit down—you're not going anywhere yet!" I reply. "The fridge door is suffering from RSI and is putting in a workers' compensation claim. The microwave is seeing a lawyer about workplace harassment. The toilet, which has taken an unprecedented hammering of late, is suing for divorce. The bathroom is already in counselling and yet, in these unprecedented times, moving forward together, in this once-in-a-lifetime event, the vacuum cleaner has seen no work for over 6 weeks! It's developed a Liverpudlian accent! I heard it weeping last night..."

"You mean sweeping?" asks the List-Maker. I ignore her fatuous comment.

"... weeping last night. It feels unloved, unwanted. It has even signed up online to 'Lonely Household Appliances Looking for Action.com'. It has met a toaster from Ukraine and transferred $3000 into the toaster's bank account for airfares—apparently. This morning, I overheard the bins talking—yes, there is an unpleasant smell in the air—the smell of mutiny! There's talk of a strike and a public demonstration. They have a leader, an instigator, an agitator, leading their crusade—Yosemite Bin Laden—a garbage tyrant."

"That's absolute rubbish," says my daughter.

"My thoughts, exactly! Just because you're both at home, one pretending to work, the other pretending to study, it is not an excuse to absolve yourselves from all household duties. To end on a positive note, I say this; I have myself, full confidence that if all do their duty, if nothing is neglected, and if the best arrangements are made, as they are being made (by me), we shall prove ourselves once again able to clean our home, to ride out the storm of infection, and to outlive the menace of tyranny and lack of toilet roll, if necessary, for years, if necessary, alone. That is the resolve of my governance, my family - every man, woman and child of them. We shall go on to the end, or until it's time for bed.

We shall clean in the house, we shall clean on the seas and oceans, we shall clean with growing confidence and growing strength in the air, we shall clean our plates, whatever the cost may be. We shall clean on the beaches, we shall clean on the landing grounds, we shall clean in the fields and in the streets, we shall clean in the hills and in the laundry (not forgetting the downstairs toilet). We shall never surrender!

And lastly, I'll say this; never in the field of human conflict was so much owed by so many (you two) to so few (i.e. me)."

"Are we done here?" asks my daughter. "I've got a video to upload to TikTok."

"Not quite," I reply. "There are still the PowerPoint presentations to get through explaining what a dishwasher does. I've also drawn a map which will help guide you both to the washing line and back in a safe and timely manner."

"Whatevs bro," she replies. "PM me!" She disappears out of the room without a care in the world. The List-Maker, who has busily been scribbling away throughout my brilliant and stirring oration, hands me a list.

"The sole on my favourite pair of boots has come loose. Can you superglue it? And there are still holes in the fly-mesh which need fixing, and what with all the rain we've had lately, the grass is getting a bit long." She stands and walks away. "Oh, I almost forgot..." I live in hope "I've volunteered you for meals on wheels delivery for the old folk at Quarantine Towers, so you may get a call later today from Maureen Grimbreath, so don't be alarmed." The dog finishes its noisy, but seemingly enjoyable, thrice daily ablutions, and toddles off out of the room following the List-Maker... not before dropping a carpet bomber which singes my nostrils and instantly fades the curtains. I'm left alone. I wonder if Winston Churchill ever encountered this response. Strewth! How can I fly like an eagle when surrounded by dodos? The shed and a glass of chilled white wine beckon once I've finished cleaning the kitchen.

Saturday

Another terrible night's sleep. An old woman dressed in a giraffe costume stabs me with a plastic peg outside the OK Corral. As I lie dying, she stands over me and whistles the tune to 'Raindrops Keep Falling On My Head,' and asks me if she's missed the last bus to the cemetery gates. Steve McQueen picks me up and inserts me, rather roughly, onto the handlebars of his Penny-Farthing. We travel through the hills for hours as the life drains out of me, and my prostate takes a battering. He's in the wrong film and I bloody-well let him know. It doesn't go down well, and he throws me off a cliff into a burbling river. I wake with a start and stare at the revolving ceiling fan for ten minutes. The clock tells me it's 4:30am. I idly wonder whether Eric Clapton has ever cleaned the pan after making poached eggs? Egging nightmare! I may as well get up and put some washing on.

Chapter 31

Some Better Days

Monday

I'm sitting at my computer staring out into the garden, thinking of nothing... again. Bored and delusional, I decide to pay some bills. I find last month's electricity bill email and open it up. It's only 3 weeks overdue, but what the heck, I'm in a generous mood, let's get it paid. I scroll down to the amount owed for March. Shiver me timbers and slap my arse with a wet Cod! I come over all faint as my head swims in some surreal film directed by Ingmar Bergman starring Ernest Borgnine and Kylie Minogue. Surely this is a mistake? They must have got me mixed up with someone else. My eyes begin to bleed, and my left leg involuntarily stiffens, then quivers in a non-sexual way.

I'm pretty confident, right now, Queen Elizabeth II will be opening *my* electricity bill from "Green Clean Dirty Coal Energy," and will smile with glee. "Oh, golly gosh, we have made a saving this month. I did remind Phillip to turn off the convector heater in the arboretum once he'd finished throwing hand-grenades at the palm trees. But I suspect it's a joint effort amongst the 300 servants which achieved this marvellous outcome." She informs her private secretary, Tarquin-Smythe-Soiled-Trousers-Sycophant the 4th, to reward all the household staff with an extra humbug in their wage packets at the end of the millennium.

Tuesday

I'm still reeling, and seething, about the electricity bill. I know full well who the culprits are. The List-Maker and my daughter (aka—snowflake millennial). I call an urgent family meeting. When no one, bar me and the dog turn up, I call another one. Still nothing. I turn the modem off. Within 10 seconds, my audience awaits. I give them a lecture about cutting back, saving money, reducing heating costs. It's an unprecedented time and we need to flatten the curve—especially of the bloody electricity bill!

"When I was a lad..." I begin. My daughter looks up from her phone, momentarily.

"No, please, not the 'when I was a lad' speech again. We've heard it a hundred times before. It never improves," she yawns. Undeterred, I march onward.

"When I was a lad, when it was cold, we put on another layer of clothes..."

"Sorry to interrupt," interrupts the List-Maker, interrupting, "but how many 'Fs' in, inefficient?" she asks, as she scribbles into her bloody notepad.

"Two," I say. "Why?"

"No reason," she responds. What the hell does she mean by that? By now, my daughter has left. Apparently, she's having a "Zoom party" with Katy Perry tomorrow and needs to tell the world. Obviously, it's far more important than my dwindling bank balance. "You realise having 3 of us at home, one working, one studying and one... ahem... doing something else, will increase all our household costs?" says the List-Maker, unhelpfully. The fact she emphasised the words *doing something else* has not gone unnoticed. It's like gambling... sometimes, when you're losing, it's time to cut your losses. I give up... for now.

Wednesday

I'm staring at a blank screen... again. I have a new idea for a book. It's about a shoe salesman from Sheffield who accidentally meets Sophia Loren back in the mid-sixties. There's a chemistry between them. Sophia is a Hollywood superstar, a screen siren, a vixen smouldering with sexuality. Colin Biggins sells work boots and "Kiwi" boot polish from the back of his knackered Ford Cortina. He's also quite good at snooker, with a top score of 47, off the break—mind. They both meet in an all-night café and share a Spam sandwich and a cup of Bovril together, and love is born. A rough outline of the plot is completed but I decide to sleep on it—I don't want to get sucked into another black hole of cul-de-sacs, one-way-streets, dead-ends and dark tunnels from which there's no escape... a fate worse than reading a Jeffrey Archer book... hang on... what the hell was I on about? I've lost my thread...

Thursday

The List-Maker is downstairs in her "working from home" office—Netflix going full pelt, earphones on, singing Whitney Houston's "I Will Always Love You" ... she's obviously met someone online. Probably Jeremy Boringdom from Canada, who owns half of the Rockies. He's a multibillionaire, Angus Cattle stud breeder with significant interests in coal, iron ore, gold and knitting patterns from Iceland. Good luck... I'd love a night out with that wanker—not! My daughter is in her bedroom, supposedly home studying.

"Hey, Dad!" she yells. "Do you want to speak with Katy Perry?" She's in a state of great excitement—my daughter, not Katy Perry. I'm in my office next door, trying to figure out how Sophia Loren came to be in a greasy-spoon café in Sheffield, at 11:30 pm on a cold Wednesday night back in 1965.

"No! I bloody don't want to speak to Katy Perry!" I yell. "Although, if her dad Fred Perry is there, I'll have a word with him. The last polo shirt I bought from him cost me £80! When I was a lad, you could get two for £10!"

"My God! You're such a loser!"

Sometimes life throws you a pleasant surprise. I'm in the kitchen wondering what delicacies to prepare for our evening meal, and as with a lot of things lately, I'm drawing a blank. The List-Maker enters and tells me she's cooking dinner tonight. WTF! Once the paramedics depart and I've had a stiff brandy, I smile at her.

"Okay," I reply, thinking it might be a prank. "Would you like me to give you a crash course on how to use the oven and stovetop? They're not as complex as they appear."

"Ha-ha, you're not funny," she snipes as she leaves the kitchen. "Oh, by the way, could you knock together a Greek salad to go with it?" she shouts back.

"Of course," I reply, pinching myself to make sure this is not another one of my weird dreams. Nope! It's definitely reality. With salad prepared, I retire to the living room to watch cooking shows interspersed with rolling news coverage. After two hours my wife calls out informing me that dinner is about to be served. I nearly bump into my daughter as she comes hurtling down the stairs.

"Did I hear correctly?" she pants. "Has mam made dinner?"

"Yep! You'll remember this day for the rest of your life. It's like a JFK or a John Lennon moment. Everyone remembers where they were when those two were shot."

"Who the hell is JFK? Is he some rapper I've not heard about? And who's Jan Lemon?"

"Don't they teach you anything at school?"

We both wait expectantly at the dinner table for our gourmet surprise to be presented to us. Plates and cutlery are dispensed, the Greek salad is in place.

"Come on, the suspense is killing us. What have you made?" I badger the List-Maker. She smiles at me in triumphant fashion, as though she's just invented the vaccine for COVID-19.

"Tonight, we are having baked potatoes!"

Friday

Ahh, the serenity. The List-Maker is working from her 'real' office and my daughter is studying at her boyfriend's... or so she says. I hope sex education is not on the curriculum today. My life returns to normal. There are no demands on my time, no snacks to make, no dishes and pots to collect, no washing to hang out. Why can't life always be like this?

It's no good! After two months in lockdown, my mojo has deserted me. On a good day, I used to knock out 7000+ words, on a bad day, at least 2000. Today, my first day with no distractions, I've managed just 12 words, 14 if I include the comma and full stop. I'm not even sure it needs the comma. I read somewhere it takes 30 continuous days to form a habit or break a habit. After 60 days I've accumulated a multitude of bad habits and lost all my good ones.

I list all my unhealthy habits, hoping by putting them down on paper, I'll be able to confront them. Bad Habits: reading rants on Facebook, watching people fall over on Facebook, watching pranks on YouTube, watching Game Show bloopers on YouTube, drinking way too much coffee and tea, waking at exactly 4:30 am every morning and not being able to get back to sleep, forgetting to shower, forgetting to shave, forgetting what day it is, staring into the garden for hours on end without even thinking about anything, forgetting to ring my mother and sister, drinking too much white wine, drinking too much white wine way too early in the day, forgetting to write, not being able to write, watching too many cooking shows and rolling news coverage, not exercising, wondering about ridiculous things like "how do they put air into a ping-pong ball?" I feel depressed looking at the list and redress the imbalance by writing down my good habits.

Good Habits: erm... ahem, okay, here we go, good habits, good habits... hmm. Aha! Yes, almost forgot... the baby oil and visiting my favourite website and... wait, no! That's not a good habit! It should definitely be on the bad habit list—at the very top!!! I decide it's a stupid exercise in the first place and rip my lists to shreds.

Saturday

I've always had lucid dreams. They usually involve me trying to evade gangsters, falling off tall buildings, desperately searching for a toilet or getting it on with a throng of dancing girls dressed as nuns—sometimes all at the same time. Tonight is no different.

I'm on the roof of a skyscraper. It's not a sleek modern one built from steel and glass. It's a cross between the Empire State Building and Notre Dame Cathedral, and it's in a shocking state of disrepair. Don't ask me what I'm doing on the top of this building or how I got there... I'm as surprised as anyone to find myself in such a predicament. There's a way down. An exceptionally long pair of wooden extension ladders are perched precariously at the front of the building. The type of ladders your local window cleaner used in the 1970s i.e. wonky, unstable, a death trap. I've never feared heights, but as I gingerly lower myself over the edge and place one foot on the rung, I get a panic attack. I'm so high up there are clouds below me. To make matters worse, I only have one hand free. My right hand grips a rung, my left holds onto a cup and saucer full of black tea. I like a nice cuppa more than anyone, but not on top of a 1500 ft extension ladder. Now the wind gets up... of course it does. Not so much as a whisper of a breeze all day. Once I'm on the ladder, "Hurricane Widow Maker" hits!

The ladder creaks and groans as it twists and turns. I cling on for dear life. To add insult to injury, I spill at least half my cup of tea without so much as a sip. The inevitable happens and I fall. Miraculously, I somehow survive. The next second I'm scampering through Target desperately looking for a toilet, hoping I don't wet myself before I find it. A gaggle of Nuns pull me into an alcove and disrobe. Yes, I've hit the jackpot—my lucky night! Then Robert De Niro, Al Pacino and Joe Pesci appear clutching baseball bats. Give me a break! I know this will not end well!

I've been staring at the ceiling fan for over an hour. It's 4:30 am. Counting sheep just makes me agitated. Okay, I've hit rock-bottom and there's only one thing left to do... something I swore I would never-ever-ever do again after my first and only harrowing experience. These are desperate times. I switch the bedroom light on, sit up in bed and grab my Kindle. I unlock it and navigate to a Jeffrey Archer book. Sure enough, two pages in and my eyelids droop, my breathing becomes deep and heavy, and blissful sleep wraps a blanket around me.

Chapter 32

Here We Go Again... Again

Well, here we go again. When I began writing this week's nonsense, I was a free man. By the time I finished it... I am no longer free. In a few days, I will enter full lockdown again... aargh! Someone pass me a bottle of poison, a handgun and a fucking bullet! I really thought I'd never need to write another 'Lockdown Diary Blues', again. (I bet some of you are wishing the same.)

The List-Maker never returned to work and has been working (???) from home all this time and will be at home for at least the unforeseeable future. Today is my daughter's last day of physical schooling, as of tomorrow, she'll also be home-schooled for six weeks, followed by 2 weeks' holiday followed by... well, who knows what.

I'm not sure of your exact circumstances, but for a good proportion of you, I suspect you're going through a similar nightmare. Well, now is not the time to drop one's head. Onwards and upwards. In the immortal words of Winston Churchill, "We shall fight them on the beaches, we shall fight them in the streets and supermarket aisles. We shall never surrender the toilet roll or tinned tomatoes. This will be our finest hour!"

Naughty NASA

Apparently, NASA has discovered a new constellation, or so the newspaper headlines screamed a few weeks back. It seems the geeky boffin heads spotted a new zodiac sign hiding behind the Sun. It's named - Ophiuchus. It runs from November 29 to December 18.

I've spent all my life in the false belief I was a Sagittarian, only to be now told I'm an Ophiuchusian. I was fond of being a half-man, half-flying horse, half-biscuit, holding a bow and arrow—that's pretty cool. Now I'm an old man wrestling with a snake, at least I think it's a snake, if it's not, then he has a serious genital deformity and it's not wrestling he's engaging in.

A quick scan of the well-respected website, 'Signs of the Zodiac for the Gullible & Desperate', tells me as a Sagittarian, I was honest, compassionate, independent, curious, emotionally intelligent and could play 'Hey Jude' on the bagpipes whilst balancing a pineapple on my head. Now, as an Ophiuchusian, I have an explosive temper, I'm jealous, secretive, egotistical, and sexually magnetic (at least they got one thing right). I also like to dress flamboyantly and wear a lot of pink and turquoise plaid. It makes me sound like the Scarlet Pimpernel on crystal meth! If I saw a person with those personality traits and dress sense walking towards me, you wouldn't see me for dust.

The revelation of a new constellation sent the astrological world into meltdown. They soon wheeled out a spokesperson for the 'Astrology, Tarot Cards & Face Painting Guild.' The spokesperson was understandably livid with NASA. The space agency, in one fell blow, had completely dismantled her belief system, not to mention her lucrative revenue stream. She said, "I wouldn't take much notice of what NASA has to say. After all, they're certainly no experts in astrology." Which is true. They are, however, experts in a "real" science called "astronomy" which uses mathematics, physics, and chemistry to understand celestial objects and the universe. I know this can't compare with reading tea leaves, feeling the bumps on your mother's head or dividing 6 billion people into 12 neat groups, but then again what can?

Next, it was the turn of NASA to trundle out a spokesperson who wearily replied, "This is an old story which was doing the rounds about six years ago. The Babylonians studied the stars and planets 3000 years ago and they knew there are, in fact, 13 constellations, not the current 12 astrology uses. They chose 12 because it was mathematically neater, i.e. 12 constellations at 30° gives you the 360° of the ecliptic." Kaboom! The NASA spokesperson had "lit up" the astrologists, big time. Never pick an argument with an egghead. Furthermore, NASA's website stuck the knife in deeper. They categorically state, "Astronomy is a science. Astrology is something else. It's not science." Smackdown and game-over red rover! So, it turns out it was all a storm in a teacup. NASA went back to work figuring out how to grow parsnips on Mars and the astrologists polished their crystal balls and shuffled their Tarot cards wondering why they hadn't seen that one coming.

This brings me neatly onto horoscopes. Occasionally I'll read my horoscope, usually when I'm bored to death and want a cheap laugh. I'll do this online and pull up at least 3 different sites to see if the horoscopes align with each other, after all, they should. Alas, they rarely do. To be honest, the predictions are so vague and woolly you could interpret them any which way you wanted. "You will go on a long journey, it could be physical or metaphysical, either way—be prepared—take a cheese and onion sandwich with you. Remember to be generous in spirit, if not in kind, and it will be returned to you tenfold... or possibly thrice. If a friend offers you a Werther's Original, proceed with caution. Your lucky word for the day is, bumfuzzle." WTF!

I've yet to read a horoscope specific about upcoming events. Just once I'd like to read something like, "Listen, pal, if I were you, I wouldn't get out of bed today. I see a runaway steam roller careering down a steep hill. At the bottom is a blue Subaru Forester, as flat as a fucking pancake—you drive a blue Forester, don't you? At 7:32 pm or possibly 7:45 pm, you'll burn your spatchcock because you forgot to put the timer on. Just before bed, you'll shout at the dog for breaking wind and stub your big toe on the table leg.

Of course, only if you avoided the steam roller. Don't say I didn't warn you!"

Chapter 33

An Offence Of Karens

F or those of you whose birth name is Karen, I apologise in advance. For those of you who have been living on the Moon for the last few years, let me explain. The term "Karen" is typically applied to a white, privileged, middle-aged, middle-class woman who takes it upon themselves to complain aggressively to staff or managers in fast-food restaurants or service stations. She is not passive-aggressive, she's active aggressive and usually bangs on about her rights and democracy, or if American, the constitution, of which she usually knows very little about.

Pre-Covid, her rants were usually saved for the hapless staff who take orders at KFC or McDonalds. Post-Covid, she has lifted her game, somewhat. She now vents her spleen about face masks, social distancing, and vaccinations to anyone in her line of vision. It seems Karen is perpetually pissed off! She will deliberately go out of her way to take offence at someone or something. When she is taken to task on this, she reverts to a 3-year-old and throws a hissy fit, tantrum or wobbly— sometimes all at the same time.

Back in the good old days, people like Karen were known as dickheads. It didn't matter what gender, age, colour, or demographic they came from. A dickhead is a dickhead is a dickhead.

According to the omnipotent geek ball in the sky (Google), the male equivalent of a Karen is a "Kevin", or a "Ken", or a "Darren" and even possibly a "Richard", although, I'm not sure where the last one came from.

Obviously, a disgruntled ex-wife of someone named Richard. But for now, let's split the difference and call him Garren.

Garren is the interfering old stick insect who writes letters to his local newspaper each week;

"What is wrong with the young people of today? In my day, when we passed a sexagenarian in the street, we would stop and salute them while singing Land Of Hope and Glory then ask them if they needed their lawn mowing. This morning when I told two teenagers, who were loitering with intent outside the haberdashery, to get their hair cut and join the army, they told me to fuck off! The birch is too good for them; bring back hanging is what I say!"

Different countries have different ways of complaining. In America and France, complaining in public is a national pastime and a spectator sport, and I have to say, they are exceptionally good at it. In Britain, we would rather have our testicles or titties tasered than complain in public. To us, complaining is like sex—it should be done in the privacy of one's own home, or motel room. We will complain to our husband, wife, girlfriend, boyfriend, spouse, dog, hamster, bit on the side, reflection in the mirror until their ears self-combust. In public, it's a different matter. In a restaurant, if we order a slow-cooked boeuf bourguignon, with a side dish of mushy peas, and get served a shit sandwich with escargot puree—we smile politely and thank the waiter profusely. If this happened in New York or Paris, you are on the precipice of WW3 and the four horsemen of the apocalypse have just galloped into view.

If complaining was an Olympic sport, there are only two contenders for gold and silver. Sadly, the Brits would pick up the wooden spoon—not that they'd complain about it—well, not until they got home.

Britain is a nation of tribes, brought together under one umbrella. We also like a drink, in fact, we like to drink to excess—most days—and nights. We bypass complaining, sidestep arguments, but go full throttle when it comes to "kicking the shit out of one another"—of which we truly are Olympians. There's only one gold medal winner there! This is what happens when you mix Celts, Picts, Angles, Saxons, Vikings, Normans, Gavins and Pixies together. Let's face facts, we're all gobby bastards who can't handle our drink and like nothing better than a good punch up—how do you think rugby was invented?

There was a "Karen" video that went viral last week. It was "Aussie Karen". She entered a Bunnings (hardware) store, in Melbourne (a capital city in Australia, not Austria, for you Americans). Melbourne is going through a second wave of Corona and the state government brought in new lockdown restrictions and the mandatory wearing of facemasks... if you could not reasonably social distance (i.e. 1.5 m apart—this distance fluctuates depending in which country you live in, how tall you are, what day of the week it is and what you ate for breakfast—the damned virus keeps moving the goalposts).

Aussie Karen was outraged because a condition of entry was the wearing of a facemask. Now, I could have sympathised with her indignation if they'd insisted on a cavity search followed by two hours of waterboarding, but for crying out loud they were asking her to wear a facemask! She quoted some law from 1948 about human rights, how they were being infringed upon, and I quote, "As a human living woman, you have no right to ask me to wear a facemask! This is a public place! This is discrimination!"

I'm not sure why she said 'living human woman'... as opposed to what? Those sneaky shapeshifting deceased Vulcan and Dalek women? Plus, I hate to pick her up on a minor point, but I will. A hardware store is not a public place. It is a private business operating on premises it owns or pays rent on. A council park or playground is a public space. A national park or the beach is a public place. A shop, store or shopping mall is NOT a public place—it is a business. You can't walk into your local Safeways supermarket with a picnic blanket, a hamper full of egg and cress sandwiches and iced tea and fire up your barbeque.

Anyway, back to 'Aussie Karen'. The store manager and staff kept their cool (much to the annoyance of Karen, who desperately wanted to escalate things) and Karen left without buying anything—as far as I could tell. Which begs the question, why did she go in there in the first place? I guess the answer is obvious. She went into the store to take offence.

I can't remember the last time I took offence at anything, and you should see some of my book reviews. I grew up in the grim north of England and by the age of 10, it was impossible to offend, embarrass or humiliate me. When they handed out acting parts for the school Christmas nativity play, and I was given a non-speaking role as a tree—well, my humiliation and embarrassment was complete. When you've been a prop on stage, in front of your peers nothing can ever offend you again. The only way is up.

The Karens of this world have been coming in for a bit of stick lately, thanks or no thanks, to smartphones and the toxic cesspool in the ether— Facebook. But they are fighting back. They've formed a group of Karens called 'The Living Human Women Karen Group'. Yes, I know, it's an uninspired name, especially when the collective noun for a group of Karens is 'An offence of Karens.' The 'Karen Offence League' would have been a far better name, in my humble opinion. I emailed them my suggestion, and guess what? They were offended and outraged at my idea and accused me of infringing on their human rights, as living human women. They intend to sue me for harassment, slander and misspelling "irascible" (it's true—I put the "E" before the "L"). I returned fire by explaining the complexities of defamation, and they should sue me for libel—not slander. I received a very nice "thank you" email in return. Anyway, needless to say, I'm expecting a barrage of critical reviews on my books soon—even more than usual.

I understand it... I get it... we are going through tough times at the moment. Lockdowns, lack of movement, no tinned tomatoes, bog-roll rationed, disease and death—it's making everyone extremely tetchy. As we are told, ad infinitum—'we are all in this together' some more than others it appears.

What Aussie Karen doesn't get, is by refusing to wear a mask, as a condition of entry, because it violates her human rights (as a living, human woman—not a dead Aardvark woman) it may cause the death of another human woman... or man. What about their rights? Karen is oblivious to this fact or just doesn't care. There's always a small minority of humans that are different. The rules don't apply to them. How else can you explain the success of Canadian band, Nickelback or UK band, One Direction?

Chapter 34

We've Gotta Get Outta This Place

Thursday

I should be writing my next book, but I'm not. I'm staring out of the office window in despair at the ramshackle state of my garden. That's the problem with nature—it just never stops. Cut the grass, trim the trees, weed the path, de-horn the unicorn. I could rush out there right now and tackle those jobs, but I know in two weeks' time, I will stare at the same view again. As Neil Young once said, "Rust Never Sleeps". Maybe that's a poor analogy?

I cheer myself up by flicking through Facebook. I've joined some new groups lately, and I've got to say, it's great entertainment. These are local "town community" groups, created to foster a sense of community spirit, recommend local tradespeople, highlight upcoming local events (that's gone quiet) and share such helpful tips like, "How To De-flea Your Teapot" or "This day, 100 years ago, an elephant fell into the river and has never been found".

A few examples of recent enthralling posts include, "Can anyone recommend a local Laminex bench-top repairer? The wife placed a hot casserole dish on it and the rest is history." Or, "I've found a black boot on Buckland Street. If anyone's noticed they're missing a boot, PM me and I'll give you my address. I think it's size 8, or maybe 6, it's hard to tell." You get the gist. Occasionally, though, it really kicks off.

Today, there's a post from Mandy Briggs, who has lost her cat. She describes it in great detail, maybe too much detail (it has four legs, two ears, has fur and looks like a cat). She says the last time she saw the cat was at 8:45 pm last night. I find it odd that she knows the exact time she last saw her cat. It answers to the name of, "Rafferty Hornblower." Okay, stop there! If I were a cat, and my owner had given me that name, I'd also be doing a disappearing act pretty quickly. Imagine the embarrassment when she's calling you in on a night, "Rafferty Hornblower, it's din-din time." The three tough street cats from next door, Glasseye, Canine Killer and Dave would all be sniggering into their little furry paws. Anyway, I digress, back to the post about the missing cat.

It doesn't take long before a "dogfight" erupts. A guy called "Fugly" has a pop at Mandy for having a cat, and that, in his opinion, all cats should be euthanised because of their destruction of the local, native inhabitants (I assume he means birds, rodents and roaming wildebeest). Rather harsh, I think, but it is Facebook and anything goes in the safety of your own home, and with your favoured weapon of choice—a keyboard. Someone else quickly replies that "Smugly Fugly" should be euthanised. Oh boy, this is going to be good! Turn the fan to overdrive and release the shit!

It appears the community group is about evenly split; half are cat haters; the other half are cat lovers—I'm agnostic on the matter—which means I can sit back and enjoy the ensuing barrage of insults. It transpires that our tight-knit, little community, is a seething, bubbling hotbed of open wounds, old grievances, and bare-knuckled aggression.

At one point, during a particularly brutal onslaught by the cat lovers, a guy posts the following, "Does anyone know if the bakery has reopened yet?" He's obviously misread the flavour of this particular post and has blundered in, unwittingly, with eyes wide shut. It's like he's driven his tiny ice-cream van into the middle of the Battle of the Bulge. The man is ripped to shreds within seconds, from both sides. He limps from the battleground with his head in one hand and his testicles in the other.

It doesn't take long before the community group administrator, Oberfuhrer Barbara Littlegood, steps up to shut down proceedings. Barbara is the team leader of the local Girl Guides Troop and Hitler Youth Movement, respectively, and has a PhD in meddling. She doesn't take nonsense from anybody, and she immediately quashes the debate... not that it really was a debate, more like an October uprising.

Peace descends for a while, but it's an eerie sort of peace - the sort of peace you get just before a fusillade of Tomahawk cruise missiles zips past your window. Sure enough, I don't have to wait long. Someone starts a new post, with just one simple word, "Meow" and the whole shit fest kicks off once more with gusto. Ah, good old Facebook and community groups, what would we do without you?

Friday—All Day

I've taken to having a little power nap mid-afternoon, at about 1 pm (my body clock has gone to pot, give me a break). The problem is, I nod off quickly, within about 5 minutes, but then the itches start. An itch to the nose, then the ear, then the cheek, and most disconcertingly, I can occasionally feel my eyebrows growing. To feel a hair pushing out through its follicle is a most unpleasant sensation.

At the moment, my nasal hair is getting out of control. For 40 plus years, my nasal cavity was prepubescent, not a hair to be seen, as smooth as an eel. In the last couple of years, it has hit puberty big time. I think it's on a concoction of aloe vera, ginseng, fish oil, and illegal steroids. At some stage, the hair from my nose and eyebrows are going to join forces in the classic pincer movement and annex my face north of my chin. Both parties will sign a peace treaty, but I know it won't last. The axis of errant facial hair has an ultimate goal - Moscow. The only way to stop it will be a surprise counterattack by the elite guard from that distant land—Mons

Pubis. Outnumbered, outmatched, and out curled, the nasal/eyebrow axis will sue for peace, in what will become known as the Treaty of Vershair.

Weekend (they used to be enjoyable)

The List-Maker and I have different tastes in TV programmes. She prefers shows like Grand Pretentious Designs For Super Rich Empty Nesters; Escape To The Country For Bitter Divorcees; Downtown Abbey; The Farmer Wants A Subservient Housewife and a Shag; Midsomer Genocide and Gordon Ramsay's Puff Pastry Nightmare On The River Ouse.

I, however, prefer things like Peaky Blinders; Michael Caine films; British comedy shows; war films (WWII preferably, but WWI is acceptable) and of course - snooker. This can sometimes cause friction in the Northouse... house. I penned a letter to the BBC asking if they could solve this conundrum by commissioning a series set in Dorset, during the second world war, where Gordon Ramsay and Jamie Oliver are renovating an 18 bedroom farmhouse, with the help of a very charming milkmaid and Mr Bean. Throw in a couple of murders, a cat called Bruce—that can knit, a cut-throat gang of Birmingham tinkers and Michael Caine and we're onto a winner. Oh, not to forget, a final Ninja assault course, snooker challenge, between Michael Caine and Delia Smith set in a stately home. No, on second thoughts, ditch Delia Smith. That would be a ratings disaster. Replace Delia with Nigella Lawson or even her dad, Nigel Lawson. I'm looking forward to their positive response but don't expect to receive one.

Tuesday

I've just watched the news again. I don't know why I bother as it's very depressing. They've even stopped showing the obligatory "good news" stories at the end, about Panda Bears rollerskating or doing the Times crossword - things must be bad. Maybe the Pandas are also in lockdown... what am I talking about? They live in a zoo - they're always in lockdown.

A news reporter out on the street stops a man and asks why he's not wearing a facemask, as it's now obligatory. The man explains that he was born with a "genital" defect that prevents him from catching Covid-19. I assume he meant "congenital" defect, although he did walk with a peculiar gait, so who knows?

They always roll out professors or someone with a triple degree in stating the bleeding obvious, in times like these. Some egghead has done a study and has calculated that 10% of the population are stupid, which just goes to show how far removed from reality he is. The true figure is at least 33%, even I know that, and I only have a diploma in eating pot noodles.

A lot of our politicians are coming under fire at the moment, which, under normal circumstances, would bring me great joy. However, some are doing the best they can in these trying and "unprecedented" (just shoot me) times. Let's face facts; some are good people trying to do good things; some are bad people trying to do good things, and some are bad people doing nothing much at all.

It can't be easy. Imagine being elected a year ago. As prime minister, or president, or dictator (?) you thought you were going to have 4, 5, or maybe 50 years in power feathering your own nest, helping your old school chums or business buddies out, then retire from politics and take a £4.8 million job a year as head of a charitable foundation for saving the Lesser Spotted Dung Beetle of Antarctica.

Then—POW! You get Covid right between the eyes! (Not literally, although I can't be certain.) This is not how it was supposed to be for the likes of you. You were looking forward to playing golf with a Saudi prince at St Andrew's once a week. A spot of sailing on the Mediterranean on Lord Cumquickley's luxury aircraft carrier. Breakfast at Tiffany's, lunch at Raffles, and dinner at Burger King.

Well, it's all gone to shit now! You're now mired up to your neck in the real world with the rest of us plebs. You could end up stuck in your 100-

room mansion, on three-hundred thousand hectares, in rural Cornwall, for years. No more Henley Regatta and eyeing up the totty for you, my lad! No more "swiftys off the wrist" from undergraduates trying to work their way through university. Welcome to ground zero!

Well, as we are forever being reminded, this virus does not discriminate. We all have to suffer the same consequences. I guess it really is the great leveller - eh?

Chapter 35

I Get Knocked Down But I Get Up Again

Sunday

The List-Maker has called an extraordinary general meeting of the "Northouse Worker's Party Executive". This comprises me, my daughter, and the List-Maker—Chairman of State Affairs, Ultimate Delegation & Under-Salting of Potatoes. According to Chairman Maker, it's time for our yearly Spring clean. I tentatively inform her it's the wrong season for Spring cleaning, as Spring normally falls in.... Spring. This entirely justifiable quibble, aimed solely at getting myself out of doing any actual work, fell on deaf eyes.

The meeting was quickly wrapped up when the List-Maker came to her unanimous and unilateral decision. Operation Thunderbolt (The Spring Clean Offensive) would commence this coming Thursday, at 14:00 hrs, sharp. With the meeting finished, she goose-stepped out of the room, leaving me and my daughter to bemoan the forthcoming week.

This would not be our usual Spring clean, where a few things are discarded, and some half-hearted dusting is undertaken by my daughter and some slapdash repairs are made by me. No, this was going to be massive! Think of the D-Day landings and you'll get the gist. We could both see a dark, foreboding storm heading our way.

Monday

It's 4:30 am and I'm in bed, wide awake, thinking about juniper berries —as one does. When I was growing up, juniper berries, whilst not common, were available for purchase if you knew where to look. These last thirty years, they have become harder to find than rocking horse shit. I cannot remember seeing them anywhere. Nor have I ever seen juniper jam, juniper marmalade, or juniper wine. It's as though the juniper berry has been eradicated from planet Earth, and probably for good reason. If my memory serves me correctly, they tasted bloody awful, like swigging your grandmother's perfume.

I remember they were supposed to be good for you, in what sense I'm not sure. I haven't even seen them used by celebrity chefs, and they use the most outlandish of ingredients imaginable. Truffles, saffron, shitake mushrooms, eye of newt, tongue of mermaid. If it's not Jamie or Gordon imploring me to incorporate these elements into my cooking, then it's Nigella, Marco Pierre, or Wolfgang Puck (now there's a name to meddle with). They obviously don't shop at my local supermarket, which has only recently got around to stocking parsley. I'm living in the wrong town; the demographics are all to pot.

I assume the juniper berry grows on a bush, probably the juniper bush. This makes me ponder; what is the difference between a bush and a shrub? I decided that when I eventually get out of bed, I'll do some research (Google) on the juniper berry, and the differences between a bush and a shrub. With the matter put to bed, I promptly fall asleep.

Thurs-D-day

The List-Maker had pre-ordered a skip bin for "Operation Thunderbolt". It's just been delivered and is the size of a large bungalow. I imagine the Pentagon's spy satellites are already zooming in on it, trying to determine if the Northouse's are covertly moving Scud missiles across the continent. This doesn't bode well.

The Spring clean has been underway for over 3 hours. Early in proceedings, I was relinquished from my initial post as 'Sergeant in Charge of Dining Room De-clutter' and demoted to 'Acting Private Bin-Man & Tea & Biscuit Provider'.

There are three piles of rubbish growing at an exponential rate; one pile is for the charity shop, one for the council tip and one for the missile silo parked on the driveway. My job is to move clutter to one of the above.

I tackle my new position with an onrush of apathy. Things get off to a poor start when I hold up two items and query why the List-Maker has marked them for the bin. She's less than impressed and decidedly more grumpy than usual. "It's a videotape of Rolf Harris in concert at a children's charity event in 1985 and a remote control for a TV that we got rid of in 1998. What's wrong with you? All the videos are going," she states, emphatically.

"Those videos cost a fortune," I complain, thinking of the thousands of pounds I foolishly spent on buying them. Why had I not been able to see into the future?

"No one has video players anymore; we don't even have a DVD player! Videos in the bin and DVDs to the charity shop!" she snaps. I pick up an item from the charity shop pile. It's 'Hanson's Greatest Hits' CD. I flip it over and read the tracklist. Hmm, most peculiar, it only lists one song - MMMBop. I move it to the bin pile. No one's ever going to buy it. I'm not sure how it even ended up in our household. Maybe one of my girls went through a shoplifting phase?

Tip Trip 1

I'm making my first sortie to the council tip. In the old days, it used to be simple. You'd hook up your trailer, throw all the crap into it, drive to the tip and reverse to the edge of a massive hole the size of Jupiter and dump it all in there. Things have changed. Paper and cardboard in one crate; green waste to the right; e-waste in the shed; metal to the left; batteries in the compound. When my daughters were younger, they used to love coming to the tip with me. It was like a day out at an industrialised version of Disney World.

As I enter the tip, I notice a crew of workmen busily erecting the framework for what I can only assume to be a new sign. It's about the size of a football field. Why would anyone need a sign that big to write the word "Tip" on it? Maybe they're trying to attract passing aliens.

They call the tip attendant, Dave. I have mentioned him before in these missives. Nice man, but my God, he's a boring tit! Ten minutes in Dave's company and you lose the will to live. Once he starts, he never stops, and I don't have the heart to tell him to sod off like I would with most people! He has a nickname in town—'Tip of the Iceberg' because there's not much up top. My only escape route is if another unsuspecting customer arrives behind me.

I'm out of luck today. Dave rests his arms inside the passenger door and sticks his head through the window. He talks about the weather, his hernia, his dog, a documentary he watched on the feeding habits of dung beetles, his walking stick, how to make rhubarb jam (you need rhubarb, apparently) and how to extract a poison dart from the cleft of your buttock. I'll put the last one in my memory bank just in case I ever holiday in Madagascar and visit the Poison Dart Pygmies of Lardarse Land.

After ten minutes, I can feel the blood draining from me. I reach for the glove box and desperately search for the syringe full of cyanide I have on hand for just such moments. Alas, I'm out of luck. I seem to remember using it the last time I picked my sister up from the airport. To my relief, I witness some poor sap pull up behind me and I'm gone, baby!

Friday - Tip Trip 2

As I make my first trip of the day to the tip, I'm cogitating on a deep philosophical quandary. What would be worse; performing MMMbop every night for the rest of your life or flat-sharing with Dave? As soul-sapping as MMMbop is, I'm afraid Dave is the winner - but only by a nose.

I arrive at the tip and much to my surprise, Dave isn't there, which is odd because Dave is always there. There's a new attendant on duty. A very short, wiry woman. She bears an uncanny resemblance to Heinrich Himmler with a ginger afro.

"Where's Dave?" I enquire politely as I exit the car.

"Retired!" she snaps back at me. Hello... here we go. Don't break the ice with a bit of passive-aggressive behaviour, just get straight in there with a knee to the ball sack.

"Retired? I thought he was retired, already? I mean, spending your days in a small shed, with a heater, a kettle, a cupboard full of pot noodles and a pile of old porno mags is my idea of retirement." She screws her eyes up at me, inspects my trailer and hands me the bill.

"Cash only!" she barks.

I stare at the ticket. "Erm, I think you misunderstand. All I wanted to do was dispose of this rubbish, I wasn't planning to buy the land for redevelopment."

"I don't set the prices; I just enforce them." Great! Not only has she no sense of humour, but she's a bloody jobsworth. She must have Canadian and German bloodlines.

Tip Trip 3

Heading back to the tip with my third load of the day, I drive as slowly as possible and take the long route. No need to rush these things. The ambience back at Northouse Mansions is not conducive to my penchant for doing fuck all - which I've got to say - is a very underrated pastime.

The new tip attendant is preying on my mind, and I figure it's time to pull out all the stops and launch the Northouse charm offensive. It's never failed me yet... well, apart from the time I got a speeding ticket from an over-aggressive traffic cop, and the occasion a bouncer threw me out of a nightclub... oh, and the time when... well, okay, the Northouse charm is not always 100% effective, but I have a pretty decent hit rate.

I exit the car and the ageing, miniature Rhianna is immediately onto me, inspecting my trailer, recording my number plate, taking DNA, blood, and saliva swabs, clipboard in hand. Time for some witty one-liners.

Ahem... let's just say the one-liners went down like a lead-turd. Time to bring up the big guns. My funniest joke ever. It's the one about the pole dancer, the tax inspector, the furry glove, and the bucket of frogs—it never fails!

Nothing! Not so much as a titter. She mutters something under her breath. It sounds like, "smut" but I can't be sure. I realise humour is like music, food, and the Hanson's—it's subjective. Not everyone has the same tastes. She hands me another mortgage... I mean waste disposal invoice. I decide to cut my losses and unload the trailer.

Friday - Tip Trip 4

The sign for the tip is finished. It's no longer called the "Tip". It's been rebranded, 'The Bob Geldof & Greta Thunberg, Reclamation, Salvage, Recycling and Sustainability Re-Use Facility'. Catchy, very catchy. I bet the council paid a few hundred grand to some corporate city slickers to come up with that one. It even has a feel-good, by-line, 'Working Towards Zero Emissions - Saving the Planet Together'. Unfortunately, it is rather undone by the following, 'Open Thursday, Friday, Saturday, 10 am - 2 pm (excluding public holidays and severe weather)'. Saving the planet is obviously a part-time job done during clement weather. Well, you can't rush these things.

As I pull into the place formerly known as "the tip", she emerges from her shed, like a Black Widow Spider, ready for a feed, with clipboard in hand and bazooka strapped to her back. Ho, ho, she's in for a surprise! On my circuitous route to the ex-tip, I've decided upon a new tactic to win her over — I can't keep paying these ridiculous prices. At least Dave used to undercharge me or even occasionally throw me a freebie. I emerge from the car with gravitas, confidence and authority, then ruin it when I accidentally break wind. This startles her and puts her on guard. It completely annihilates any sense of moral authority I was hoping to impose and also puts a dent in the zero-emissions policy of the place. I plough on with my master plan. Now is not the time for defeatism.

"The weather's been unpredictable of late." It's my opening gambit and fails miserably, as I knew it would, especially after the accidental release.

"Hmm," is her only response, as she feverishly inspects the contents of my trailer like a border security guard on National Free Immigration Day. Okay, time for 'Plan B'. I'm going to bore the living shit out of her!

"Did you know the juniper berry is native to North America, Asia and Europe? It has many beneficial health properties, including antioxidants, anti-inflammatory compounds and can help promote heart health and combat diabetes. In traditional Chinese medicine, they've used the juniper berry for thousands of years to help flush out toxins, impurities and find missing mad women.

It grows on a Juniper tree, not a bush or shrub as some idiots assume. The term 'shrub' and 'bush' mean the same thing, unless you are a horticultural Nazi, then there are clear delineations between the two nouns.

The berry itself is not dissimilar in appearance to a blueberry, but the taste is completely different. It has a rather astringent bite to it. You may think you've never tasted juniper before, but if you've ever had a glass of gin, then the acrid, bitter taste is thanks to the juniper berry.

There are many types of juniper berry and not all are fit for human consumption. Indeed, some are highly toxic..." After five minutes, her eyes glaze over, she sports a pallor complexion and has the tremors. I think she may be about to have a seizure. I've overdone it—I never knew I could be this boring. With sudden clarity, I realise I've become Dave. His spirit has entered me—from which orifice and direction, I know not whence—but he now lives within me. I try to make amends by offering her a gift from the trailer.

"Here, take this," I say, passing her a CD. She stares at it like a zombie.

"Hanson's Greatest Hits," she mumbles in a profound state of discombobulation. Time to unload the trailer and make good my escape before I get arrested.

Tonight

Apparently... (here we go), there has been some shoddy work performed by "Acting Private - Bin Man" (me) during the offensive. I somehow threw out a perfectly good hairdryer belonging to the List-Maker, and my daughter's collection of Katy Perry T-shirts. A court-martial is being discussed in hushed tones, in the kitchen, between two unlikely allies. It sounds like I could be publicly de-frocked.

The "scorched-earth" policy at Northouse Mansions is coming to its inevitable conclusion. From the East come the Russians (the List-Maker). From the West, the allied forces (my daughter)—they both want to capture me alive and put me on trial. There's only one thing for it—retreat to my bunker (the shed), drink cheap white wine and wonder where it all went so horribly wrong.

As I sip on Sourvinegar Blanc, I realise, with the benefit of hindsight, I should have had a private plane on hand to fly me to Argentina in case things turned pear-shaped. I think I overextended myself by planting the permaculture garden last Spring and trying to learn the French Horn at the same time. I exposed my flanks—metaphorically. It could have all been so different if it hadn't been for my overconfidence, massive ego and losing the Ardennes in that fateful counteroffensive - The Battle Of The Bulge. Damn Charles Bronson and Telly Savalas!

Well, enough of the navel-gazing. Time to relax. During the 'Spring Clean Offensive' I rediscovered a DVD player and a box-set of Clint Eastwood films. I decide, tonight, I will chill out and watch them.

However, back in the 'Soviet Zone' the List-Maker has other ideas. She wants to watch 'Celebrity Dog Bake Off Bachelorette Challenge', in which 6 pedigree hounds bake a juniper cake whilst licking their private parts and urinating on a Lazy Susan. The winner elopes to Gretna Green with a hipster millennial Beagle, but before they tie the knot, she ditches him for the mongrel 'Best Man' who recently won the lotto, has a lifetime's supply of Pedigree Chum and has not had his testicles removed. Another battle lost.

Back in the shed, I'm wondering if Dave, ex of the tip, is up for a beer. Has it really come to this? After 2 seconds of reflection, I realise it's a bad idea and decide it's time for bed.

I'm ready for a good night's sleep. My head hits the pillow and I know it will only be a matter of seconds until blessed unconsciousness arrives. Unfortunately, some numpty cockwomble from across the road is throwing an illegal party. The music is blaring out and to add insult to injury he's got MMMbop on repeat! It never rains but pours. Give me strength... sweet Jesus and pass me the poisonous juniper berries to chew on.

Carry On Rewardless

Book 4

Chapter 36

I Get Locked Down But I Get Out Again

I 'm watching the early morning news. At last, I have something to cheer about! A government bureaucrat is about to explain the new lockdown restrictions—and they are being eased, maybe.

A beige man, with a beige suit, and a beige haircut, fills my TV screen. I've never been so happy to see beige.

"We are moving from stage 2.33, version 6, step 4.5 to stage 3.1, version 4 (beta), addendum 7.65—notwithstanding."

I've been hanging out for this. I'm almost salivating.

"The easing of restrictions will commence *if* the rise in reported infections over the next 18.56 hours does not exceed 10.1 over a weekly cycle or 13.7 over a fortnightly period—pro-rata.

In layperson's terms, this means cafes, restaurants, bars, pubs, and boutique shops selling pink porcelain pigs can admit a maximum of 10 patrons at any one time, as long as the indoor area is 11.27 m^2 (or greater) and social distancing of 1.5 m is implemented unless the main opening to the establishment is facing north by northeast and the humidity level is below 71% and the average overnight temperature does not fall below 6.5C over a five-hour period during a Blue Moon.

Weddings can have 14.235 attendees (including the vicar or celebrant), as long as the best-man is barred from attending or has been fitted with a police ankle bracelet to track his movements.

Funerals are permitted with a maximum of 18.72 mourners—including officials—but not including the deceased, unless the deceased has filled out a "Green" exemption form in person, and it has been verified by a Justice of the Peace, in triplicate. No exemptions will be made unless there's an exemption to the exemption.

Funerals must be held outside unless there's a spot of rain about, in which case, 25 are permitted indoors as long as no open fires are burning, which makes crematoriums off-limits unless the crematorium can operate with a low-level flame not exceeding 6 lux, which must be signed off by a chandler with at least 44 years experience.

House parties and raves are acceptable as long as they don't exceed one person per household and no Barbra Streisand or Bee-Gees records are played.

It is still mandatory to wear facemasks unless you are exempt, i.e. respiratory difficulties, incontinence, or the inability to think.

Gyms, beauty salons, and the local rub and tug parlour are still off-limits, but it's fine to travel on overcrowded public transport, attend mass gatherings on beaches and partake in huge demonstrations as long as you're wearing breathable underwear.

Each household can mix with up to five nominated friends or family for a period not exceeding 47 minutes in each lunar cycle unless their primary abode has solar panels and, or a reverse cycle air-conditioner purchased within the last six months. However, this rule does not apply to anyone who keeps pet rabbits or who eats pickled onions on a Tuesday morning for breakfast.

Schools will resume on-site learning in 2 weeks but only for years 11, 23, preps and grade 64, except students born during a leap-year, on or before, but not including the years 1921, 1995, 2011 and 2045.

Stay at home workers must continue to work from home, unless they can't, in which case they must work from home unless they can't—in which case they must unilaterally self-combust.

The allotted individual daily exercise time has doubled from 30 minutes per day to 2 hours per day, excluding Thursdays, Shrove Tuesday, and Lent. In the unlikely scenario you hear the nuclear two-minute warning, then it is permitted to walk your dog for an extra thirty minutes on that particular day—but not thereafter. It is a one-off allowance.

Essential medical appointments of a non-medical nature are allowed unless you have a tendency to stop abruptly in supermarket aisles for no apparent reason and stare disconsolately at jars of mayonnaise.

The driving of Toyota Corolla's on the last Sunday of every month is still prohibited, unless you have applied for, and been granted, a waiver from the English and Wales Football Association (this does not apply to Scotland, or if you're Scottish living overseas or in a caravan on the Isle Of Man).

Coughing, sneezing, or clearing your throat in a loud, disgusting manner in public is still frowned upon with penalties of up to 10'000 groats, 2 years imprisonment and/or a community correction order of 150 hours watching The Hairy Bikers."

Right, I'm glad that's sorted. I feel a lot better now. I can see a light at the end of the tunnel. If anyone can't follow those simple rules, they must have a screw loose.

Chapter 37

Supermarket Blues

I 'm in the supermarket, having completed my weekly shop. I have all the essential items necessary to maintain body and soul for another week. But I've slipped up again. It's Wednesday which means dole and pension day. The place is heaving. So much for the 1.5 m rule. The supermarket, in its infinite wisdom, has decided to only open three checkout tills staffed by real human beings. At least I think they're real, but who knows in these strange times we live in.

I notice most people are wearing masks, but there is an odd few who only wear them over their mouths. Possibly they assume the mouth provides oxygen to the lungs, whereas the nose sends oxygen to the brain. And there's one or two who aren't wearing a mask at all. They appear fit, healthy individuals, but who knows? They have a wild stare, you know, the one that is prevalent in criminally insane institutions, and says, 'Go on, I dare you! Ask me why I'm not wearing a mask and I'll rip your throat out, dice you up, and bury you in the backyard!' I'll keep out of their way.

The queues are horrendous. There's only one thing for it, I'll have to use the dreaded self-serve checkout. I place my basket down, pull my carrier bag out of my back pocket and struggle to attach the handle to a row of metal prongs.

'Unexpected item in bagging area,' announces the machine in a smug, posh, upwardly mobile female voice. Here we go. I'm not in the mood for yet another battle with technology.

'It's not an unexpected item, you titanium twat! It's a carrier bag. What else do you expect in the bagging area?' The machine flashes up a button on the screen.

'Do you have your own bag?' I hit the 'Yes' button.

'Thank you for shopping with Badways. Please place your bag in the bagging area.' Give me strength. I pick my bag up and place it back down. Another message flashes across the screen. 'Thank you for using your own bag. Saving the planet together.' No! Just don't. The only thing you're bothered about is your big fat profits, so cut the sanctimonious, greener-than-thou crap. I pull a tin of tomatoes from my basket and pass it over the scanner, but before I drop it into my bag, the woman in the machine pipes up again.

'Unexpected item in bagging area.' I rub the back of my neck in an agitated fashion and glance around, trying to spot the woman, lady person who patrols the area. To be honest, these days I have no idea how to address people. Get it wrong and the morally outraged brigade will string you up in a matter of seconds. I stick my hand in the air and wave at her. She's busy with an elderly man who is trying to insert his bus pass into the EFTPOS machine. Eventually, she comes to my aid.

'Ooh, she's temperamental. Is this one,' she says. 'She's always playing up. She suffers from PMT?'

'PMT?'

'Pre-Monetary-Tension. I have more trouble with her than all the others put together.' She pulls her magic card out of her pocket, flashes it across the screen, pushes a few buttons and announces, 'Right, you should be okay now.'

'Thank you. By the way, what's your official title? I don't suppose I can call you a checkout chick these days.'

'My title is an Ingress, Egress, Consumable, Merchandise, Transit Flow, Service Representative, Officer. But you can call me whatever you like, I don't care.' At last, an Ingress, Egress, Consumable, Merchandise, Transit Flow, Service Representative, Officer after my own heart. She departs to help a woman who is trying to scan the entire contents of her basket in one go.

I slide my tin of tomatoes across the scanner and place it in the bag. So far so, so good. I repeat the process with my second tin of tomatoes.

'Unexpected item in bagging area,' she repeats. I snap.

'Listen to me, you pea-brained Dalek, unless you start playing ball, I'm going to come back here with my angle grinder and give you a haircut! Do I make myself clear?' She gives me the silent treatment. I notice a mother and her young daughter stood at the adjacent machine. They both stare at me. The mother pulls the child in close to her. I try to pacify the situation by grinning at them. The little girl looks terrified and grips her mother's arm. I've remembered I'm wearing my facemask and smiling doesn't work. I've seen my reflection in the mirror when I smile with a mask on... it's not a pretty sight. I have the mad eyes of Jack Nicholson as he's smashing the bathroom door down with an axe in The Shining.

I pull the last item from my basket, a pack of toilet rolls, scan it and place it into my bag. Good, all done. I don't like to use threats of violence against inanimate objects, but on this occasion, I think it was justified. I pull out my credit card and hold it against the card reader. It spins its wheel for a few seconds.

'Sorry, card declined. Please try again,' she announces in her pompous tone. I know I have plenty of money in my account. I try a second time. 'Sorry, card declined.' I've been at the supermarket for over 40 minutes. All I wanted was two tins of tomatoes and some bog roll. Why does life always have to be so hard? I glance around for the Ingress, Egress, Transit Flow... thingy, woman, lady person. She comes to my aid once more.

'It's not accepting my card and I know I have money on it.' She flashes her magic card, hits a few buttons, and tells me to try again.

'Sorry card declined. Error code 404—insufficient funds!' shouts the machine. A momentary silence falls over the whole supermarket as everyone turns to stare at the loser with no money on his card.

'Hmm...' murmurs the Egress woman. 'Try one more time.'

'Card declined. Error code 404—insufficient funds,' announces the cow in the machine, her voice rising by at least 20 decibels.

'Would you like me to store your items for you, and you can come back later?' Egress woman asks.

'Unexpected idiot in bagging area.'

'No, thanks. It's a fifty-minute round trip and I only have three things,' I concede, defeated.

'Insufficient funds. Card declined. Unexpected loser in bagging area.'

'You need to get this machine looked at. It has serious anger issues and an attitude problem. Who programmed it, Gordon Ramsay?' The Egress woman smiles apologetically. At least I think it was a smile—hard to tell. The mother and daughter give me a wide birth as they pass by.

'Mummy, has he got the virus?' asks the little girl.

'No, darling. He has a sickness of the mind. I'll explain it to you once we get home.' I cut my losses and remove the goods from my bag, fold it into a tiny triangle and stick it back in my pocket.

'Thank you for shopping with Badways. Please remember to recycle all packaging. We only have one planet and we're all in this together–moving forward.'

'Oh, sod off!'

'Thank you and have a wonderful day.'

Chapter 38

Post-Christmas Blues

What the hell happened to Christmas? One minute I'm with the kids in the car on our way to pick up a Christmas tree, the next minute I'm staring at the arse-end of January. I feel like one of those unfortunate people who slip into a coma and wake up thirty-five years later, wondering who shot J.R. Ewing and where the hell has all my hair gone.

Mind you, I'm not a huge fan of Christmas. There's far too much false jollity for my liking. January is a far more sedate month. Although, I can't be doing with all the new year's resolution nonsense. Did you know January is named after the Roman God, Janus, (careful how you spell it— omit the letter 'J' and you're in a world of shit.)

Janus had two heads, which would come in very handy when reverse parking. One head is looking back on the year just finished and the other head is looking forward to the new year. This means 2020 is now behind us. And what a year it was; pandemic, political turmoil, cancellation of the Olympic Games, devastating bushfires in California and Australia, a massive explosion in Lebanon and to add a final toxic cherry to the cake, the Northouse's also had Christmas visitors.

Don't get me wrong, I love having visitors, as long as they don't outstay their welcome. I think fifteen minutes is long enough for a catch up with anyone... don't you? Any longer and I'm reaching for the cyanide capsules. Our visitors stayed for 10 days!!!!! It could have been worse. At least they were friends and not family. Well, they were friends when they arrived.

It changes the whole dynamic of the house. I'm not used to spotless toilets, vacuumed carpets, and cobweb free windows. It affected not only me but also my wife, the 'List-Maker'. She now had to wear clothes in the morning instead of wandering around the house naked, like a mad old hippy with cognitive impairment. So, there's always a positive outcome in every situation.

Chapter 39

Keep Cool and Carry On

I 'm in my office, gazing out of the window, pondering life. I should be writing, working on my next book, but I've hit a brick wall. Hence the pondering.

I've had a run of bad luck recently. First of all, leading into Christmas, my new, super-fast computer had about a zillion volts shot through its clacker as a rogue (as in unpredicted) thunderstorm bore down on us. I'd spent the previous two weeks transferring everything across from my old PC, setting up my bookmarks and encrypting my porn collection. Not an easy task.

As untimely as this was, more bad luck was hot on its heels. My shed fridge went kaput (that's German for 'fucked'. I'm bilingual, amongst other things). This was a catastrophic event, as it's where my alcohol supply lives. Now, I'm no electrician but I could tell there was something wrong with the fridge when I turned it off and on again (much like you would with a computer) only to be greeted with a flurry of sparks, a bang, a mild electric shock, and a new hairstyle, as the entire electrics in the house and shed switched off.

This did not go down well at Northouse Mansions as my daughter was in the midst of a shower, rinsing dye from her hair and the List-Maker was watching 'I'm a Minor Celebrity Twat—Bring Me Off Here.' There was much consternation, gnashing of teeth and some colourful words were thrown my way... as though it were my fault! Thanks to my razor-sharp mind and the ability to think coherently under intense pressure, I opened the fuse board and reset the trip switch. Peace was restored... at least for a few minutes until I went back to the shed and tried the 'on-off' trick with the fridge again.

It's strange we humans (unlike shapeshifters and wolverines) think if we do something once, and it doesn't work, if we try it again, it might work. I do this all the time, granted, mainly in my sex life, but it doesn't matter how many times I fail and end up with the same result, I still try again. I guess it's called the everlasting light of optimism... or stupidity—take your pick.

Being an industrious sort of chap and feeling a little panicky as my alcohol was no longer being cooled, I did the only thing any reasonable man would do. No, of course, I didn't call a refrigeration engineer—why would I? I jumped onto my local 'Buy, Sell, and Swap Crap' Facebook page. I spent the next thirty minutes chuckling at some of the absolute rubbish people were trying to offload. Some even wanted money for it. Used underwear, a washing up bowl, a couch with a stain on the cushions, an electric toothbrush which had only been used once (WTF!), a drone minus controller, and a birdbath with a hole in it and no stand.

Once I'd been entertained, I spotted what I was after. 'Second-hand fridge, a collector's item, £100.' Perfect. Admittedly, the seller lived an hour's drive away, but this was a big fridge and looked cool. I texted him and we arranged a pickup time. Now, to give you a bit of context; I was knackered (for non-British people, read—extremely tired, on my last legs, exhausted.) It was the day before our Christmas visitors arrived and I'd spent the last 48 hours cutting grass, cleaning windows, fixing decking, putting beds together, wallpapering the dog, and painting the cat.

At my arrival point, I inspected the fridge. It had been switched off for some time, but I'm a canny sort of bloke so I asked the seller to switch it on. When I opened the door, the light came on. Good to go!

Back at home, it took me an hour to get the thing off the trailer and into my shed. It was a heavy bugger. In the process of moving it, I managed to put my back out, scrape the skin off my knuckles, bruise my shins, trap my fingers in the door and pop a roid. As it was an older fridge (collector's item), I knew it would take a few hours to heat up and cool down... if you know what I mean. I left it for 12 hours, then inspected it. Hmm... not much happening. I gave it another 12 hours and checked again. It was now warmer on the inside than on the outside. I left it for 48 hours—still nothing. After 72 hours I realised I'd been sold a dud (hey, I'm on the money. There're no flies on me!). I texted the seller and informed him his fridge was a piece of crap, which didn't work. He sent a very polite text back, saying it did work. The light came on when I'd opened it. I sent back a slightly less polite text stating I hadn't bought a fucking fridge to entertain myself by staring at a lightbulb every time I opened the door! He sent back a very restrained text telling me I should ring a refrigeration engineer to take a look at it.

I composed a reply, but the List-Maker read it before I could hit the send button. She advised me the text could get me arrested and extradited to Guantanamo Bay detention camp and banned from Facebook and the local bowls club. As a responsible adult, I erred on the side of caution, due to the threat of withdrawal of certain privileges, and deleted the text.

So, what lessons did I learn? Don't buy a second-hand fridge from a complete git when you're tired. Don't assume because the light comes on inside the fridge, it actually works. Don't buy a fridge because it looks cool but isn't actually cool. And hey, buy a new fridge which has a guarantee, from a reputable store. You can get one for about £100!

The next day our visitors arrived... what else can I say?

Chapter 40

Life In A Goldfish Bowl

My major distraction, when it comes to writing, is the news. Not the boring news about politics, wars, and pandemics. No, the news which distracts me the most are those obscure, bizarre and frankly, unbelievable stories. I kept a note of the more memorable ones over the last month... so here we go.

It's official. Humans now have less attention span than goldfish, which apparently can focus their mind on something for 9 seconds. Humans dropped to 8.8 seconds. Hang on a minute... I need to check Facebook and make myself a coffee.

That's better. Now, where was I? Oh, yes, concentration. Humans now have an attention span of 8.8 seconds, which I find hard to believe. Whenever I speak to my daughters or the List-Maker about anything, I get about 4 seconds to make my point before their eyes glaze over and they retreat to the cupboard under the stairs.

Apparently, there has been a 33% drop in human concentration since... well, since the last survey they did, although no one seems to remember when that was. Now it's payback time for the much-maligned goldfish.

On an evening Mr and Ms Goldfish can sit around the fireless gas fire carping about their day. Inevitably, talk turns to their son, Gill.

'I'm worried about him,' Ms Goldfish laments, as she knits a barnacle.

'Why?' father asks, as he tries to smoke his pipe, which for some reason keeps going out.

'He has the attention span of a human. He'll get nowhere in life. I can see him spending the rest of his days with us in this glass bowl. I wanted him to get and out and see the world, meet a nice tuna girl and settle downstream.'

'Don't worry, dear. It's just a phase. Your brother, Fin, was the same for a few years and now look at him—he owns the largest scented candle store in the whole of Fish Creek. As a business idea, I'm surprised it took off, really.'

According to the article from whence I got this information, the reason for our diminishing concentration is 'the digital world', or in particular—smartphones. They state that 77% of people aged between 18—24 reach for their phone when bored. Sometimes up to 150 times per day. This compares to only 10% of people aged 65+ reaching for their phones when bored. This I can understand. There's no point picking up your landline to find out the latest news on Glen Miller because it's a dumb phone and knows nothing... that and the fact Glen has been missing for 76 years doesn't help either.

It's a nice story (the goldfish comparison, not the Glen Miller one). And that's exactly what it was—a story. Various reputable news organisations debunked it as fake news.

Chapter 41

Zoom Zoom Zoom

I t was inevitable. With the rise of Zoom, remote learning, and online meetings, it was only a matter of time. I'm surprised it took this long.

A sad sack in the USA is going through a bit of a rough patch at the moment. My heart bleeds for him. It really does. It could happen to the best of us... or the worst of us. He is (or was) a high school teacher. Because of covid, the kids were remote learning, and he was teaching them via Zoom. He finished the lesson and signed out. As he had a bit of spare time on his hands before the next lesson, he did what any self-respecting man would do and put something else in his hands whilst looking at his favourite website (and it wasn't the Dow Jones Index).

Unfortunately for him, and his previous class, who could still see him on their screens, things went a bit pear-shaped. I abhor crudity, so for those who are dim and not following this thread, I'll try to put it as politely as possible. He was caught on camera choking the chicken... bashing the bishop, if you know what I mean? Oh my God! There's always one who doesn't understand. Let me explain. He was visiting Sister Palmer and her five lovely daughters, shaking hands with the milkman, feeding the chucks, polishing the bannister. Great! At last, you've got it! Well done!

His defence was that he genuinely believed he'd signed out of Zoom. What he does in his free time is up to him. I'm sure most schoolteachers mark essays, prep for the next day, scan their diary to see how many pupil free days they've got coming up (which surprisingly always coincides with a public holiday). This guy obviously had more pressing matters on hand...

or in hand. The upshot is he's been stood down pending an investigation. I'd think that would be the least of his worries compared to telling his missus why he's not logging on to Zoom anytime zoon... I mean, soon.

Chapter 42

Don't Overfeed The Chucks

G ood grief! Another story about self-abuse. I blame it on the pandemic and the amount of time couped up in your luxury 80-bedroom mansion. If you're easily offended and prone to impotent outrage... hang on, that's the entire world, isn't it? I digress... but if you are —skip this next segment.

A guy working in a warehouse depot was caught on a security camera having a swifty off the wrist, you know, burping the worm, paddling the pink canoe. Oh no! You... the dim one, please don't make me go through all this again. It's the same solo activity as above. Pray, let me continue? Good.

When his boss pulled him into the office to discuss the misdemeanour, the guy got all abusive and threatened him. The boss terminated his employment. As disconcerting the incident was in the embarrassment stakes, it's only the start of the story.

The guy (let's call him the compulsive wanker), instead of swallowing his medicine and going quietly (and possibly asking for a good reference as a cocktail shaker), takes the boss to the Ombudsman for 'unfair dismissal'. Come on? Really? The whole situation is embarrassing enough. Wouldn't any normal person want the least amount of publicity possible? I use the word 'normal' in the broadest sense.

The wanker and the boss end up at the tribunal. The wanker's defence was that there was nothing in his contract of employment about not knocking one out in the warehouse depot. I can only imagine the new contract of employment if he'd won the case.

Contract Of Employment

Working Hours: 7.30-4:30 pm

Morning Break: 10-10:15 am (15 minutes)

Lunch Break: 12:30-1:00 pm (30 minutes)

Duties: Load and unload vehicles

Safety Responsibilities: Wear PPE at all times while in the warehouse. Intervene when witnessing unsafe practices.

Prohibited: Wanking whilst on duty or during meal breaks is severely frowned upon and could lead to premature firing. Save it for your home office, bedroom or shed, or if you're from London—Hampstead Heath.

You'll be pleased to know (or maybe not) the judge found in favour of the boss. Why? Because the Wanker didn't get sacked because of wanking. He got sacked because he'd been violent and aggressive towards the boss when he accused him of wanking. What the right hand giveth, the left-hand taketh away.

Chapter 43

Bloody Harry

As much as I like to search for nuggets of unusual news, it's become harder over the last month. The reason? Bloody Prince Harry and Princess Merkel. It's everywhere, the two of them and their sidekick, Oprah. As much as I love to hear about Royal millionaires and billionaire Hollywood celebrities complaining about how hard they've got it, the truth is, I've had a gutful.

Their dilemmas have been chewing up front pages and the 'shares' on Facebook all over the world. The whole saga bores me witless. But I'm confused. Okay, I accept Harry is a 'Ranga', which by default means it's hard to pull a girlfriend at the best of times, but why is he banging a German Chancellor who is 66 years old? He's not a bad looking lad. Surely, he could do better? I know he once dressed in a Nazi uniform for a fancy dress party, but please, cut him some slack. We all do stupid stuff when we're 18, or if you're a member of the Royal Family, when you're 68, or 79 or...

Hang on, that's Google and Facebook's 'so-called news' for you. I retract everything I said—unconditionally. Apparently, he's married to Meghan Markle (a Hollywood 'C' actor) not the mother-in-law from hell in the Fatherland—Angela Merkel. One vowel, one misplaced letter, an easy mistake to make. My apologies. Here's a conundrum to end on; why are men with ginger hair called 'ginger', yet women with ginger hair are called 'auburn'?

Chapter 44

Sir Jamie Of Oliver

We all love Jamie Oliver... don't we? What's not to love. We've watched him grow up in front of us. He has a Cockney energy about him that makes you want to retire to a desert island. No, truly, I like Jamie. He's done some good things over the years, and I believe he's a well-to-do-geezer.

'Awright, my son? Do leave it out, darling. Knock it on the head. Biff, bang, wallop, what a picture, what a photograph, whoops Mrs Brown, how's yer fancy? I'll walk darn the Strand wiv... yer father? Stick it in yer family... album.'

Apologies, I had a bit of a head spin for a moment. I watched too many Dick Van Dyke films as a child. I realise 1'ooo Americans have just unsubscribed as they reckon, I need some care and attention in a high-security facility. But for all my British readers still reading (barring ginger London Royalists), let me continue.

Where was I? Ah, yes, Jamie and the attention-grabbing headline which caught my eye.

'Viewers outraged and disgusted with Jamie's Pizza Topping!!!!'

What the hell had the governor of Celebrity Chefs done to deserve such a headline? My mind was boggled. My flabber was gasted. I was discombobulated by the power of 10. What was the topping he put on his pizza dough?

My mind was in a feverish, frenetic frenzy. With this amount of outrage and disgust, it must have been something sensational, possibly even career-ending.

Did he curl a long one out, much akin to a Walnut Whip, dumped strategically between the olives and salami? Maybe he forwent the tomato paste smear and vomited last night's vindaloo onto the base? A dead rat? Cat shit? Boris Johnson's toenail clippings? Nigella Lawson's earwax? The answer to all the above is 'no'. He put grapes on the damned thing. Give me strength and strike a light!

Chapter 45

Supermarket Blues... Again

I seem to spend half my life in supermarkets. I'm in there so often I'm on first-name terms with all the staff. In fact, last year they invited me to Safeway's Christmas work function. Unfortunately, I couldn't attend as it clashed with my nasal hair trimming night.

This morning, as I made my way towards the supermarket entrance, an elderly lady stepped out in front of me. We did the old two-step shuffle. As I took one step back, so did she. As I moved forward, she followed suit. This continued for quite some time. I'd still be there now if I hadn't grabbed the bull by the teats and taken radical action. I kept completely still and held my arm out, indicating for her to move forward, playing the consummate gentleman. As she shuffled past, she called me a 'Bloody dickhead.' Charmed, I'm sure. When you get to her age, I suppose you don't give a flying shit anymore. I'm looking forward to old age. I'm going to become the complete bastard I've always aspired to be but never had the balls to do so.

I don't hate shopping, only shoppers. A supermarket aisle is not the place for a good old natter with your next-door neighbour whom you only saw twenty minutes ago. Then there are the aisle hoggers, or as I like to call them, selfish, inconsiderate, brain-dead, wank-goblins! These are people who leave their trolley slap bang in the middle of the aisle as they peruse what flavour lightbulbs they're going to buy. I'm too polite to say,

'Oi, noggin, shift your trolley,' so I employ a little schadenfreude. The first thing I put into my trolley is a large pack of condoms, extra small. No, my sex life hasn't suddenly done a 180. Be patient and read on. When I come across an aisle hogger, I discreetly drop the prophylactics into their trolley and cover it up with another product. Occasionally, when I've nothing better to do, I'll deliberately hang around and surreptitiously watch as the person makes their way to the checkout. It makes for grand entertainment, but then again, the List-Maker has told me on many occasions to 'grow up and get a life.' Maybe she has a point?

This little ploy backfired spectacularly one time when I didn't meet any aisle hoggers and forgot about the condoms in my trolley. An elderly checkout girl (that doesn't make sense) remarked,

'Don't worry love, it's not what you've got, it's what you do with it.' Considering I don't do very much with it at the best of times, it was cold comfort for my embarrassment. I tried explaining they weren't for me, they were for my best friend, but it only made matters worse.

Chapter 46

Recipes

The List-Maker brought a book home the other night, The **Downton Abbey Cookbook**. I was bemused, to say the least. The last thing the List-Maker cooked, a decade ago, was a pot noodle. It turned out to be a disaster as she baked it in the oven. Hell of a mess to clean up.

As I'm the main chef, cook and bottle washer at Northouse Mansions, I flicked through the cookbook to pick up some recipe ideas for the weekend.

Peasant on Toast: wonderful as a supper—remember to remove their hobnailed boots before cooking. You don't know where they've been.

White Swan with Marmalade Broth: if you don't like marmalade, replace it with unicorn quince.

Albino Tiger Testicles in a Red Wine Jus: simply delectable! The downside is, you only get two per serving. A rare delicacy—even rarer now!

Hairy Badger with Fig Jam: delightful! Although, be ready with a toothpick and a box of tissues after you've finished.

Tasmanian Tiger Terrine with Waldorf Salad: pretty hard to make these days as Waldorf's are hard to come by.

Chapter 47

Fairy Tales

Y et again, I wake at 4 am... on the dot and cannot get back to sleep no matter how many times I mentally sing 'Mr Bojangles'. Instead of doing something useful, like rising to work on my next book, or spray-painting the dog a rainbow colour, I lie in bed and think about Jack and the Beanstalk, and Hansel and Gretel, as one does.

When I was about six years old, I received a gigantic book of fairy tales for Christmas. It had all the usual stories in there; Snow White and the Seven Vertically Challenged Individuals; The Plain Duckling; Beauty and the Primate; Ali Baba and the Forty Kleptomaniacs. I'm being politically correct lest I outrage or offend anyone.

The two I found the most disturbing were Jack and the Beanstalk, and Hansel and Gretel. Although, to be honest, they were all sinister, macabre, and bloodthirsty. I think it's why I enjoyed them so much. They all had a hidden message they were trying to convey, but I'm not sure all of them managed it.

Let's look at Jack and his unfeasibly large beanstalk. Here is a single parent family doing it tough—mother and son. We don't know what happened to the father as it's never mentioned. Maybe he was a long-distance postman, or possibly he ran off with the local butcher, or he may have been killed in a pickling factory malfunction, or perhaps... anyway, forget about the father! He's not important. Sorry, I didn't mean that. Obviously, the father was important at some stage, and I'm sure he was sorely missed. What I meant to say was; he isn't important to the story. I'm glad I've cleared that up.

Jack is depicted as a typical teenager, i.e. feckless, lazy, indolent, churlish, and dense. The mother is a hard-working skivvy with a wart on the tip of her nose, halitosis, and terrible fashion colour coordination (now we know why the father's not around). Things get so bad that one day the mother decides it's time to sell their cherished dairy cow, Colin. The mother gives Jack implicit instructions to take Colin to the local farmer's market and get a fair price for it.

Okay, let's back up a little. If you didn't have two brass farthings to rub together, would you entrust Freddy Fuckwit to sell your last remaining prized possession, Colin? Thought not.

Jack meets an old crone on the way to the market and swaps Colin for three magic beans. What was going on in the boy's mind? Possibly he was partial to a bowl of three-bean soup. Who knows?

Not surprisingly, his skivvy mother is less than impressed with Jack's business acumen. She throws the beans out of the window, gives the lad a damn good thrashing with a broom handle, and sends him to bed with no supper.

You've got to read this in the context of the times it was written. Today, beating the shit out of your offspring with a wooden pole is frowned upon. Nowadays, Jack would be sent to his room to have a long hard think about his actions and his PlayStation would be confiscated for an hour.

The next day, Jack is up early. It's hard to sleep when you've got an empty belly, five broken ribs and a ruptured testicle. To his amazement, he sees a giant beanstalk outside and decides to climb it. Personally, I'd have picked the beans, sauteed them in a little butter and thyme with lemon juice and eaten them for breakfast on a slice of toasted rye... but that's me.

Jack hops off at the top of the beanstalk and spots a castle in the distance. If I remember correctly, (which I probably don't, as I haven't read the book since I was six), the old giant was fast asleep, and Jack stole his bags of gold and scarpered.

The next day Jack climbed the beanstalk again and stole a magic harp... I think, or am I mashing my fairy tales here?

This time, the giant smelled Jack, not literally—just a faint miasma in the air was all he noticed. Hardly surprising, considering Jack probably hadn't washed for several years. He'd have been a bit on the nose, as they say.

It turns out the giant is not only a grumpy old sod, but he's a cannibal—to boot. If he catches Jack, he's going to make bread out of his bones. I'm not sure that would comply with the food hygiene, preparation, and storage laws of today, but hey, he's a giant, who's going to argue with him?

The third and last time Jack goes up, he snatches a goose that lays golden eggs. The goose, for reasons never explained, seemed quite content living with a cannibalistic giant in a castle and kicks up a hell of a ruckus, waking the giant up. By the way, giants sleep a lot. I suspect they're overfond of the bottle and a few reefers, and who can blame them?

The giant is getting a little sick of this Jack Shit character and chases him down the beanstalk. Even though Jack is slightly incapacitated by holding a huge, squawking, golden egg-laying goose under his lazy armpit, he manages to get down first. He chops the beanstalk down with an axe (it was lying around—very handy), and the giant falls to his death. Jack and his mother live happily ever after.

Right, I have a few issues with the story. Firstly, my sympathies lie with the local undertaker and gravedigger. Trying to jemmy a giant into a coffin made for an averaged sized human is fraught with problems. I'd be on the phone with my union rep straight away. As for the poor old gravedigger—he turned up thinking he was going to dig a hole for Stumpy McHumpty—the illegitimate son of Toulouse Lautrec and the famous Russian dwarf gymnast, Mrs Grasshopper the Third. The gravedigger is going to be pretty pissed off when he finds out it's Larry Large, he's digging a hole for!

Secondly, you can't go around chopping trees or giant beanstalks down. You need a council permit. And how come Jack has spent the last thirteen years of his life as a bone idle, dimwit, and suddenly he's a swashbuckling, Pierce Brosnan, James Bond type character?

There are a few other anomalies in the story to deal with, such as stealing, murder, interfering with native birdlife without a consent form, and vomit-inducing body odour, but I'll turn a blind eye to those for the sake of brevity.

However, I don't like the ending. The fact Jack and his mother live happily ever after leaves a sour taste in my mouth *(where else would a sour taste be left? Ed)* There's something overtly incestuous about the whole thing.

Aha! But it wasn't the last we heard about Jack. He starred in the sequel —Jack the Giant Killer. It appears Jack had developed a taste for knocking off innocent giants going about their mundane, daily business. As usual, the police were never around when you needed them, even with a serial giant killer on the loose. This brings me neatly onto:

Hansel and Gretel

We start off with more undercurrents of incest as a brother and sister decide to go for a walk together in a dark wood (highly unlikely). They realise they may not find their way back home (so why go?) and devise a cunning plan. They leave a trail of breadcrumbs to follow should they get lost. A lot of the children in these stories weren't the sharpest hooks in the tackle box. There was no way they were ever going to invent the first combustion engine down the track. Anyway, I digress.

The children get lost (ta-da) and can't find their way back home (ta-da) because the local bird population have been gorging on the breadcrumbs. The children stumble upon a quaint little cottage made from gingerbread nestled in the middle of the woods. How the homeowner ever got a building inspector to sign off on a gingerbread house is another story, or at least it should be.

A more pressing question is how come the birds were happy to feast on paltry breadcrumbs when they could have been tucking into gingerbread? Questions that forever remain unanswered.

The cottage is occupied by a cannibalistic elderly woman named Syphilis the Great. She can't believe her luck when two slightly rotund children turn up on her doorstep. (There seems to be an awful lot of eating people in these fairy tales—but each to their own.) The old crone is having a cracking day! Earlier in the morning, she'd offloaded three beans in exchange for a fat dairy cow, which went by the name of Colin, from a slovenly, smelly, halfwit, named Jack.

Anyway, to cut a short story even shorter, the old gammer locks the children up in large birdcages hung from rafters. She quickly sets about building a roaring fire in her oven while cackling away at an extremely annoying volume.

Hansel and Gretel are going to be on the menu tonight. In fact, they're the Chef's Specials. Somehow, Hansel grabs an old bone, which has an uncanny resemblance to the humerus of a young child (it's not funny) and unlocks his cage.

Meanwhile, the old crone is still poking and prodding at her hot oven (no, no, no! It's not a euphemism—good grief, some people's minds are forever in the sewer!)

Jack jumps down... hang on, I've become slightly discombobulated... ah, that's right, *Hansel* jumps down and gives the old bag a kick up the arse sending her headfirst into the roaring fire. He quickly slams the oven door shut and slides a bolt across it.

I'm not sure he needed to bolt it shut. If you've been kicked into a roaring furnace, which could melt plutonium, it's hardly likely you're going to be in a fit state for a spot of infanticide and cannibalism, even if you should clamber out. Apologies, I digress again. Back to the story.

What happened next? You guessed it... Hansel and Gretel lived happily ever after, together I assume. To me, the moral of the tale is obvious; don't hang out with your sister, it can only lead to trouble.

I actually did some research for this piece of gibberish. It's true! I consulted the "know-it-all" in the sky—Google. When I typed "Jack and the Beanstalk" into my search engine it brought up a list of book reviews. It was a mixed bag. People either loved it or hated it, with a vengeance. One reviewer took great exception to it. He ranted on about what a terrible book it was, and it was teaching children it's okay to steal. He said if he should ever meet the author, he would murder him. Next, he quoted one of the ten commandments, 'thou shall not steal.' The irony of his words was not lost on me. You must not steal, but it's all right to murder an author who has been dead for over three hundred years (if that's possible) because you didn't like his book. He gave it a one-star. I've had some pretty nasty one-star reviews in my time, but I can't beat that. No one has ever threatened me with death after I'm dead... if that makes sense.

Another reviewer accused the book of ruining his life as it was responsible for his addiction to alcohol and Class A drugs. Clarification: I'm still talking about Jack and the Beanstalk, not my books... let's not get confused here. I'm sure some of my books have caused mental anguish to people in the form of extreme boredom, but I'm pretty certain they never pushed anyone over the edge. Well, apart from myself... and possibly the List-Maker.

Who would have thought a story whose first incarnation appeared in 1734 would still raise such ire today? If my books are still receiving one-star reviews in 2321, I'll die a happy man.

Chapter 48

Baby You Can Drive My Car

My blood pressure has been through the roof lately. This is not because of a poor diet or lack of exercise. It's down to stress. Daughter No.2 has been learning to drive for quite some time. I say 'learning' but what is there to learn? Apparently, she knows everything there is to know about driving. I'm not a great passenger at the best of times, no matter who's behind the wheel, so every outing is stressful.

'I've told you before; it's mirror, signal, manoeuvre,' I yell.

'That's what I did,' she screams back even louder.

'No, you didn't! You did it in reverse. Manoeuvre, signal, mirror!' I notice something peculiar about her feet. 'Please tell me you're not using your left foot to brake with?'

'Yes, why? It's how I've always done it.'

'You use your right foot! That way you come off the accelerator and onto the brake. Your left foot is for the clutch, only.'

'Oh, shut up. What difference does it make?'

She has a tendency, when navigating a corner, to veer across the centreline. This can be rather exhilarating when a fifty-tonne juggernaut is coming the other way and you're doing 80 mph. Strangely enough, daughter No. 1 was the opposite. She used to drive in the gutter. If there was a pothole within a twenty-mile radius, she'd seek it out. Occasionally, and for reasons never fully explained, she'd sometimes discard with the road altogether and ride along with two wheels on the pavement. Isn't it funny how two offspring who have been brought up the same can have such different idiosyncrasies? They're so cute. Back to daughter No. 2.

She wants to go to the supermarket to get some alcohol for an upcoming party, but my shattered nerves have had enough, and I tell her to head home. The driving lesson ends as she zooms into the carport like Lewis Hamilton on crystal meth and slams the brakes on—with her left foot. My blood pressure falls. I've taught her, as a safety precaution, to always leave the car in gear. That way, if the handbrake should fail, the car won't roll. However, you're supposed to put the car in gear after you've stopped the engine. Blood pressure back up and another heated argument.

But all good things must come to an end... or so they say. She passed her driving test on her first attempt. This means two things; I no longer have to endure white-knuckle rides clinging onto the passenger seat whilst reciting the Lord's prayer. And secondly, what sort of slack-jawed moron would issue her with a driver's licence?

The List-Maker, who was busily cleaning fluff from her keyboard, delegated me to buy our daughter a present as a congratulation. I bought her a £200 gift card from the local panel-beater. Needless to say, this didn't go down too well with anyone. There's no pleasing some people.

The List-Maker was in a bit of a state a few days later. Apparently, she'd run a red light. Easy to do when they're changing colour. I was reliably informed by Dave at the tip (whom I get most of my information from), the police show a bit of leeway on such occurrences. The List-Maker was a little vague on the details, but I told her not to worry. Nothing will come of it.

It, therefore, came as a mild shock when I opened the infringement notice a week later related to the running of a red light. *I* was issued with a fine, so steep, I'll need to re-mortgage the house, plus 3 demerit points... on *my* licence. Once the paramedics had removed the defibrillator and headed off, I made myself a strong mug of whisky. I was suitably outraged, incensed, and slightly fine-curious. I re-read the infringement notice again. The traffic light had been at 'red' for 32 seconds!

After a hastily convened family meeting, involving the List-Maker, daughter No.2 and Gullible Gilbert here, I got to the bottom of things. The List-Maker was taking our daughter to a party whilst listening to loud Abba music on the car stereo. As they neared the traffic lights, daughter No. 2 asked the List-Maker to head to the supermarket so she could purchase alcohol for the party. This random and intensely complex request completely threw the List-Maker's concentration and hence the traffic infringement notice. After a bit more heated discussion between Thelma and Louise, they concluded it was actually my fault. Of course, it was. If I had stopped off to get the alcohol when my daughter had first asked, none of this would have happened. It's time for the shed and a yard of wine.

Chapter 49

Is There Life On Mars?

I t seems your average billionaire is no longer happy here on planet Earth. I can sympathise with them; life must be tough trying to keep up with all the noughts on the end of your bank balance. I have the same problem except my noughts don't have a positive number preceding them.

Bezos, Branson, and Musk (great name for a jazz-funk band) are shooting for the stars. Some people argue the billions they are spending on space travel to leapfrog the final frontier is disgraceful, considering the state of the world they are leaving. I'm not sure what they mean? Didn't we eradicate world hunger, poverty, disease, and injustice in the 1960s? What's wrong with the naysayers? If three egotistical man-boys, worth a collective $400 billion, want to twat about in space—let them.

Musk wants to go to Mars. Bezos wants to build space stations. And Branson, well, I think he just likes to get his grinning mush on our TV screens.

I think they're all setting their sights too low. What's the old quote, "Shoot for the stars and if you miss, you'll still end up on the moon" or over the moon.

I have a better idea: shoot for Jupiter. It's the only planet big enough to contain their massive egos. Of course, comprising mainly of highly flammable gases, they'll need to be careful when lighting their celebratory cigars on touchdown, although it would provide a visual spectacular for the rest of us plebs back on Earth.

Elon Musk has been quoted as saying he wants to die on Mars. I'm sure it could be arranged. He's not trying hard enough. Meanwhile, Buzz Lightyear... I'm sorry, I meant Richard Branson came out with one of his typical smiley, tone-deaf platitudes. He said he wanted to see the day when people of all ages, backgrounds, gender, or ethnicity would have equal access to space. Brilliant! Sign me up... there is one small caveat, though. Tickets for a joy ride on Branson's Virgin Galactic VSS Vanity spaceship cost $260'000. I'll have two tickets, please. I'll take the List-Maker with me. Although, she gets travel sick after five minutes in a Subaru. I'm not sure how she's going to cope with blasting off into outer space. I assume they provide sick bags wedged next to the in-flight magazine offering duty-free perfume. If the worst comes to the worst, we can drop her off on the moon. She can do her Zoom meetings from there. The internet connection will be better than it is at Northouse Mansions, that I can guarantee.

I'm surprised Mark Zuckerberg doesn't want to be a space cadet. He could use his Facebook engineers to design a spaceplane overnight. The wings would be on upside down and backwards, the cockpit would be on the outside, the passengers would dangle from a basket under the fuselage, and it would run on Ribena. Of course, no one could ever enter the craft because each night the engineers would move the door... because they can.

As both of my avid newsletter readers are aware, I perform a lot of research and fact-checking whilst putting this drivel together. Sometimes it can take over ten minutes. This is not a "billionaire bashing" exercise. We all know it's good to have billionaires. It's called the trickle-down effect. The process by which billionaires spend a lot of money on toys and large houses. This employs many people. Therefore, the money trickles down to everyone. Well, not everyone. But if you manufacture luxury ocean yachts, spaceships or own a dealership selling Rolls Royce cars, I'm quite sure you've enjoyed the trickle of money down your trouser leg. I remember a certain British, female Prime Minister talking about the trickle-down effect and how it benefits all of society. The trickle takes time, though. Call me impatient, but I've seen glaciers move faster.

But to be fair to the much-maligned billionaires, they do dabble in philanthropy. There are a bunch of selfless, super-rich who are always telling anyone who will listen, about their charitable donations. For some peculiar reason, they typically make these donations to their own foundation. Why don't they give fifty million to the Red Cross, Amnesty International, the World Wildlife Fund or the Northouse Foundation for a Struggling but Highly Talented and Humble Author? These organisations have been running for years and are experts in wealth redistribution. Why go to the trouble of creating a new one? Hmm... I'm not a cynic, a sceptic —yes, but a cynic—no. I am led to believe, (from Google) that charities don't pay tax and get many other benefits from governments and local authorities.

If it were a choice between paying 50% tax on my spare 5 million or giving the 5 mill to charity, I could see the benefit of helping a charity... especially as it's my charity and I decide where the money goes and reap all the kudos. But surely all charity is ultimately beneficial?

In the 10 years up to 2017, £4.8bn was donated to higher education in the UK. Now, what's wrong with that? Well... £2.4bn of the money went to two universities, and it wasn't Salford and York but those bastions of diversity, Oxford, and Cambridge, and they're hardly short of a bob or two.

Some of you will think this is the politics of envy. It's not. I'd hate to be a billionaire. You wouldn't know who your true friends were. Do they like me because of my personality or because of my money? As I don't have any friends or money, or much personality for that matter, these are questions I don't need to answer. It truly is a blessing.

But there's always the exception to the rule. Take Bill Gates and his missus. His charity has helped save millions of lives through his donations to malaria research and polio vaccines. But I'm not keen on Bill and it's nothing to do with his charity work. I dislike Bill for the fact I've been using the Windows operating system for the last 30 years. Three years of my life has been lost waiting for my computer to boot up. All you Apple fanboys and girls out there will be shouting at your iPhones right now.

"Ditch Microsoft and buy an Apple Mac. You'll never look back!"

I've been sorely tempted over the years, as I'm led to believe they're super quick, reliable and can even hang your washing out and milk your goats for you at the same time. However, having once owned an iPod, I quickly lost patience with the need to re-enter my username and password every twelve seconds. That and the fact everything is proprietary. Once you enter their ecosystem, you are their prisoner. The other thing that puts me off is you need to be a billionaire to afford anything they make.

But back to Elon Musk and his boy's own intergalactic space adventure. Elon wants humans to colonise Mars (who else is a contender to colonise Mars—sea horses? Elephants? European water voles?) Elon can see the day when planet Earth is a frazzled husk, barren of life, a celestial dust bowl spinning aimlessly around an angry Sun. All that is left standing is the Empire State Building, the Eiffel Tower, and Bradshaw's fish and chip shop on the corner of Melancholy Avenue and Bleakly Road, South Sheffield. It will be like the final scene in Planet of the Apes. But Elon's foresight means the human race will live on.

Unfortunately for him, the only people living on Mars will be about another hundred billionaires. Who's going to iron his cornflakes in the morning? It certainly won't be Branson or Bezos. Or perhaps Branson's grandiose dream will come true. What was it? Space travel should be available for all, whatever age, gender, background, or ethnicity—pass me that sick bag, now! So, there is an ulterior motive to his words. We will need an army of skivvies on Mars to clean up after the billionaires. But by then, I'm sure we'll have robots to perform all the boring tasks in life like washing up, weeding the cat, and watching Downton Abbey re-runs.

Of course, it will make one of the greatest songs of all time seem obsolete. Every time David Bowie's Life On Mars comes on the radio and he gets to the chorus and asks, "Is there life on Mars?" One hundred gloating billionaires will shout back,

"Of course there is, David! We're living proof, living the dream!" Well, it's life... but not as we know it. Beam me up, Scotty!

Chapter 50

Zebras—It's Not Black and White

I've noticed some weird events recently. I think the big tech giants (Facebook, YouTube, and Google) are spying on me and it all started with the zebras. I'm not into conspiracy theories. We all know the earth is flat, the moon landings were fake, Covid doesn't exist, and Hugh Grant has an amazing acting range (damn, bugger!)

About two months ago, I awoke in the middle of the night thinking about zebras, as one does. I spent thirty minutes convincing myself they must be the most idiotic creatures on the planet. What was God thinking when he created them?

God has spent six days creating heaven and earth, and he's due a well-deserved rest on the seventh day. I'm not sure what he did on the seventh day. If it had been me, I'd have gone down the pub and got merry. Although, I'd need to invent the pub first, then beer, and landlords... but that's a mere trifle compared to a world, right?

Unfortunately (for God), Monday morning comes around and it's back to work. Even God doesn't like Mondays, not just Bob Geldof. God now has to give all the animals in the world a colour, something he omitted when he first gave them life.

'Next,' God says. An antelope trots up. 'Name?'

'Antelope.'

'What colour do you want?'

'Erm, where am I living?'

'Africa.'

'Could you be a bit more precise? It is a rather large continent.'

'The Serengeti,' God huffs.

'Oh, excellent. I've heard the food is fantastic and that it's an exceptionally good neighbourhood. Everyone gets along wonderfully, by all accounts.'

'Hmm... I wouldn't bet my house on it. What colour do you want?'

'I think a delicate fawn colour. Perhaps with a hue of whitish-grey.'

'Next!' A pair of lions walk up, looking hard and cool. 'Name?' God demands as he scribbles on his clipboard.

'I'm Clarence and this loser next to me is Leo.'

'Who are you calling a loser? You're the loser,' Leo says, appearing most hurt.

'Can you two stop your petty bickering,' God shouts.

'Ooh! Someone's feeling frazzled today,' Clarence begins.

'You wanna watch your mouth, geezer, we're king of the beasts,' Leo adds with a cocky swagger.

'I'm God and I created you. Now stop wasting my time. I have a lot to get through and I have a dental appointment at 4:30. What colour do you want to be?'

'I was thinking a golden brown colour, with a jet black mane, you know, something that will attract the ladies,' Clarence replies.

'Yeah, I'll have the same,' Leo says.

'You can't have the same as me! Pick your own colour. I think aubergine with a pink mane would suit you.'

Leo ponders for a moment. 'Really? Hmm... you could be right.'

'Listen, blockheads,' God says, 'it's one colour fits all. What's it to be? Golden brown and black mane or aubergine and pink?'

'Ahem, golden brown and black.'

'Next!' Eventually, after a long day, God gets to the last animal.

'Name?'

'Zebra, but you can call me Equiferus, all my friends do.'

'Colour?'

'I've had a devil of a time mix and matching with some colour swatches and was getting into a real lather. Nothing seemed to suit me. Some colours made me look fat, others made me look ill. I was quite struck on fuchsia for a while, until my good friend, Fred, suggested black and white stripes.'

God places his clipboard on the ground as he rubs at his eyes. 'Black and white stripes... I see.'

'Yes, but if you could change them to a sort of chevron shape for my bottom, I'd be much obliged. I know it's a little risqué, but I think I have the pizazz to pull it off. Has anyone ever told you that you have lovely hair? Grey is the new black. But you really need to do something with it. Fred is good with the scissors if you ever want a modern cut.'

'God, give me strength,' God laments. 'You do realise you're a herbivore?'

'So, what of it? I hope you're not being discriminatory?'

'No, simply pointing out the bleeding obvious. There are a lot of carnivores around this neck of the woods and they like nothing better than chewing on a herbivore. Black and white stripes are going to stick out like the lions' bollocks.'

The zebra laughs. 'Oh, don't you worry about all those big, macho carnivores. It's all show and bluster with them, a sign of insecurity. Me and Fred intend to invite them over for supper and a meet and greet once we get our own place. We'll have them eating out of the palm of our hooves.'

'More like eating your hooves,' God mumbles under his breath. 'Okay, have it your way; black and white stripes it is.'

'Oh, and don't forget about the chevrons on my butt. It's my best feature,' the zebra giggles. 'And get yourself a modern haircut. Just because you're old doesn't mean you have to let yourself go. You're quite attractive... for an older divinity.'

'Jeez,' God sighs as the zebra prances off into the distance. 'It's the last time I build a universe. It was the wife's idea. "It will keep you occupied," she said. "A man needs a hobby," she insisted. Never again, Lord... never again.' God relaxes into his reclining, vibrating armchair, pops a Werther's Original toffee into his mouth and kicks off his flip-flops.

As the sun sets, Leo and Clarence finish licking their balls under the one tree on the Serengeti.

'Oi, Leo, you getting hungry yet?'

'You bet. I could eat a donkey... or a horse... or an antelope or a wildebeest or a...'

'Yeah, I get your point. I'm peckish myself. Problem is, I haven't spotted anything within range. There's a herd of zebras, over there,' he says, pointing with his paw.

'Where?' Leo asks.

'Look... see the mountain in the distance? The black and white throng with chevrons... it keeps moving. Got to be zebras.'

'Oh, yeah! Bit of a trek though. Must be 5 miles or more. Mind you, I do like zebra fillet for dinner. You up for it?'

'Nah, too far. Tell you what, we'll send the women. They enjoy stalking and shopping.'

'Fair enough,' Leo says as he slumps back down onto the dusty ground. 'Hey, you know the overly camp zebra...'

'Who? Equiferus?'

'Yeah, that's the guy. Pretentious git. Anyway, he and his friend have invited us around for supper tomorrow night, followed by a game of Mahjong.'

'What's on the menu?'

'What do you think?' Leo chuckles.

'Zebra burgers?'

'Yep, and ribs.'

'Okay. Sounds like a plan. It will get us out of playing Mahjong. Hate the game. What's wrong with poker?'

'I hear you brother, I hear you.'

You may wonder what all this has to do with the tech giants spying on me *(nah... who would ever think that—Ed)*. Well, about six hours after lying in bed contemplating zebras, I happened to pay a visit to YouTube to watch the show I'm recommending below. On my suggested watch list was a guy called Jordan Peterson. I'd never heard of him, but apparently, he's a clinical psychologist and public speaker who some people find contentious. Now here's the interesting part, the clip that was recommended was called The Zebra Story. Spooky, eh? *(It's called coincidence—Ed.)* At that point, I had told no one about my zebra thoughts, that's all they were—thoughts. Can YouTube now read my mind? *(No! Ed.)* I know the tech giants listen to me as not long after mentioning to the List-Maker that we need a new washing machine, or air-conditioner (for example) and hey presto, Facebook shows me ads for washing machines and air-conditioners.

Anyway, back to the zebras. A team of scientists were studying them, trying to conclusively prove why zebras are black and white. But they were having a tough time. Whenever they picked a zebra out to monitor, it would move, and they couldn't tell where it was because they all looked alike. So, they daubed a handful of zebras with red paint on the rumps to help identification. Guess what happened? The lions killed them *(Who? The zebras or the scientists? Ed)*. This is when the boffins realised the zebras' camouflage is protecting the entire herd. When lions hunt, they pick out their intended prey before launching their attack. This is extremely difficult to do with zebras because once they move, they look like every other zebra. That's why lions will pick out a young or injured zebra, or one with a red splodge on its rump because it is noticeably different from the rest of the herd.

So, the motto of the story is, if you don't want the lions to get you, blend in with the herd. *(Well, we got there in the end, but I'm not sure it was worth it—Ed.)*

Lets Keep In Touch

If you enjoyed this book then you have just read the best pieces from my free monthly newsletter. If you wish to keep up to date with my book news, there are a few simple ways to be notified. You can subscribe to my entertaining (subjective) monthly "**Discombobulated**" newsletter. This not only keeps you abreast of new releases, but occasionally I have a free book to giveaway or promotional discounts. The newsletter is designed to entertain, with short, pithy takes on the world and life... mostly my life. There's no hard sell and I won't be inundating you with spammy "buy, buy, buy" nonsense – which I personally detest. You can sign up by following the link below, which will take you to my website.

I would like to subscribe to your newsletter.

Alternatively, you can go to the following sites and click on the "**Follow**" button.

Amazon

BookBub

Facebook

For paperback readers, the links above won't work no matter how many times you tap your finger on the paper. Below is a manual link to type into your browser.

https://www.subscribepage.com/author_simon_northouse_home

If you enjoyed this book, then *reviews* are greatly appreciated. If you wish to contact me, my email address is: **simon@simonnorthouse.com** I enjoy a friendly chat, and will always reply.

Also By Simon Northouse

The Shooting Star Series

Arc Of A Shooting Star (Novel)

The Resurrection Tour Diaries (Short Story)

Catch A Shooting Star (Novel)

Fall Of A Shooting Star (Novel)

What's It All About... Geordie? (Novel)

Nuts At Christmas (Novella)

Eggs Unscrambled (Novel)

I Will Survive (Novel)

Bells At Christmas (Novel) – November 2021

The Soul Love Series

Soul Love (Prequel Novella)

Love Is The Goal (Novel)

Love On A Roll (Novel)

Love Of The Coal (Novel) - Due in 2022

The Discombobulated Newsletter Series

Keep On Keeping On - Book 1 (Novella)

Keep Karma and Carry On - Book 2 (Novella)

The Lockdown Diary Blues - Book 3 (Novella)

Carry On Keeping On - Book 4 (Novella)

Discombobulated Boxset 1 - Books 1 - 4 (Novel)

❧⤜⤜⤜ ⤛⤛⤛❧

The School Days Series

The School Report - Before We Were Tsars (Novella)

The School Report - The Final Term (Novella)